The Terror Birds

Written by Linda Chapman
Illustrated by Dylan Coburn

Collins

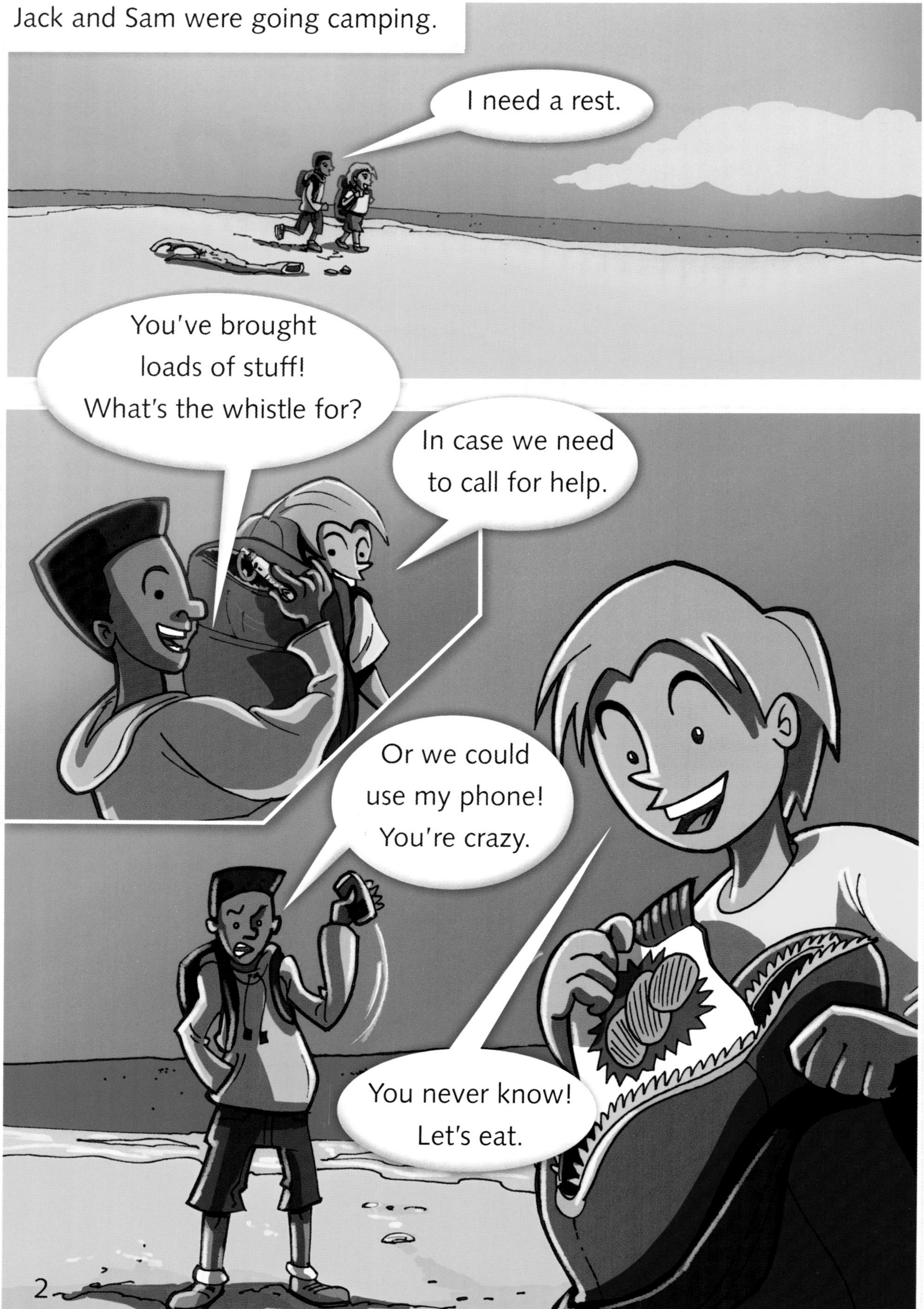
Jack and Sam were going camping.
I need a rest.
You've brought loads of stuff! What's the whistle for?
In case we need to call for help.
Or we could use my phone! You're crazy.
You never know! Let's eat.

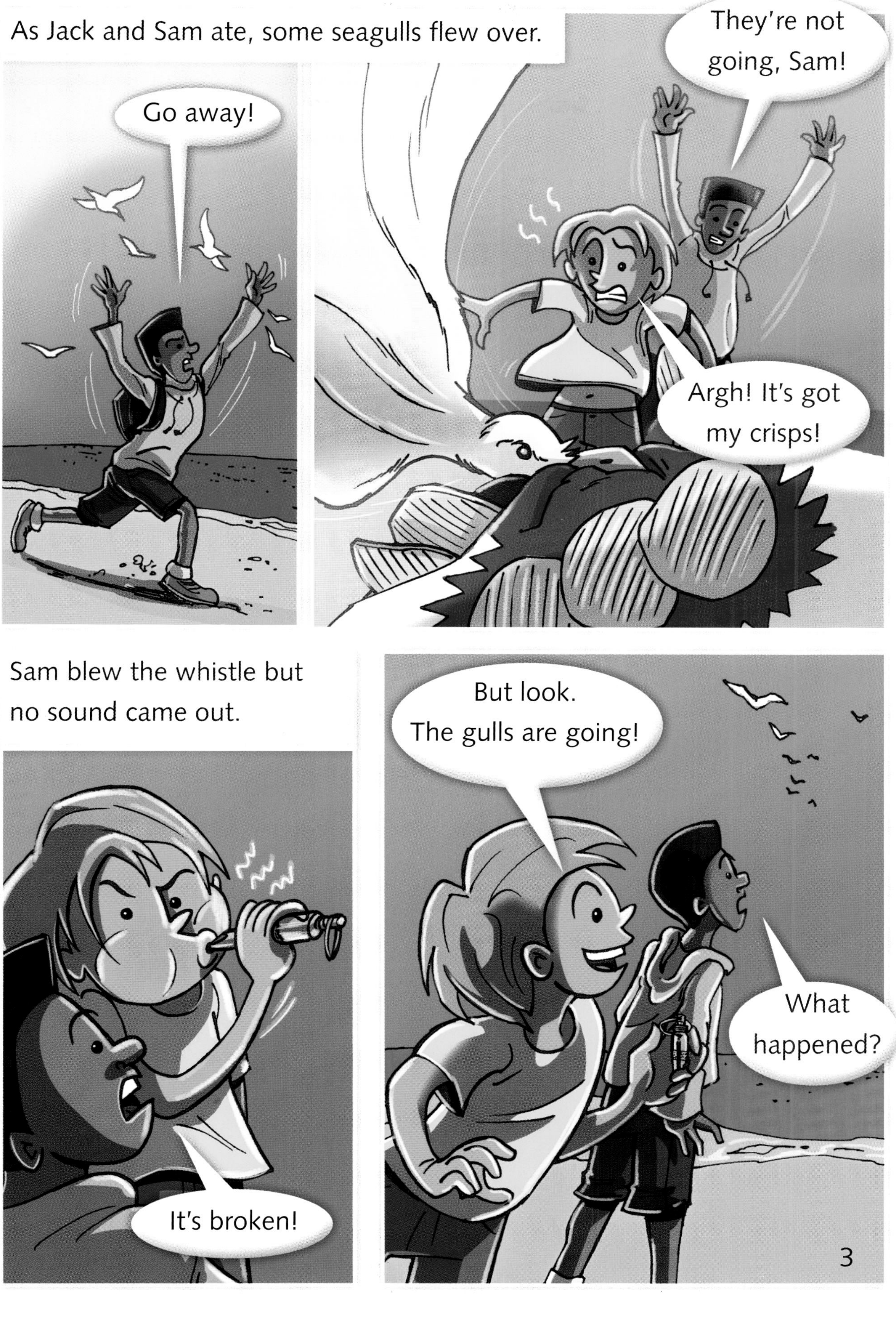
As Jack and Sam ate, some seagulls flew over.
Go away!
They're not going, Sam!
Argh! It's got my crisps!
Sam blew the whistle but no sound came out.
It's broken!
But look. The gulls are going!
What happened?

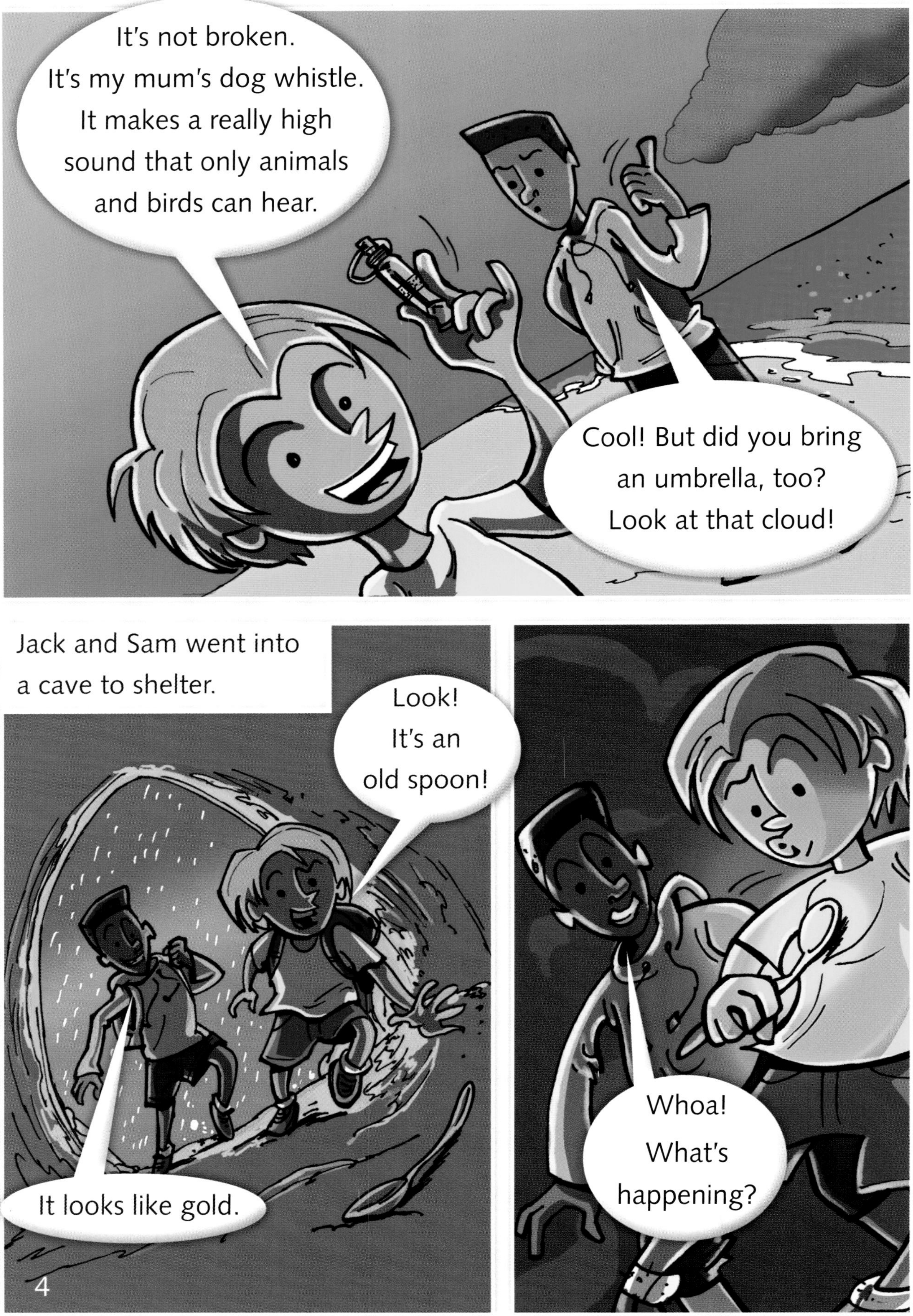
It's not broken. It's my mum's dog whistle. It makes a really high sound that only animals and birds can hear.
Cool! But did you bring an umbrella, too? Look at that cloud!
Jack and Sam went into a cave to shelter.
Look! It's an old spoon!
It looks like gold.
Whoa! What's happening?

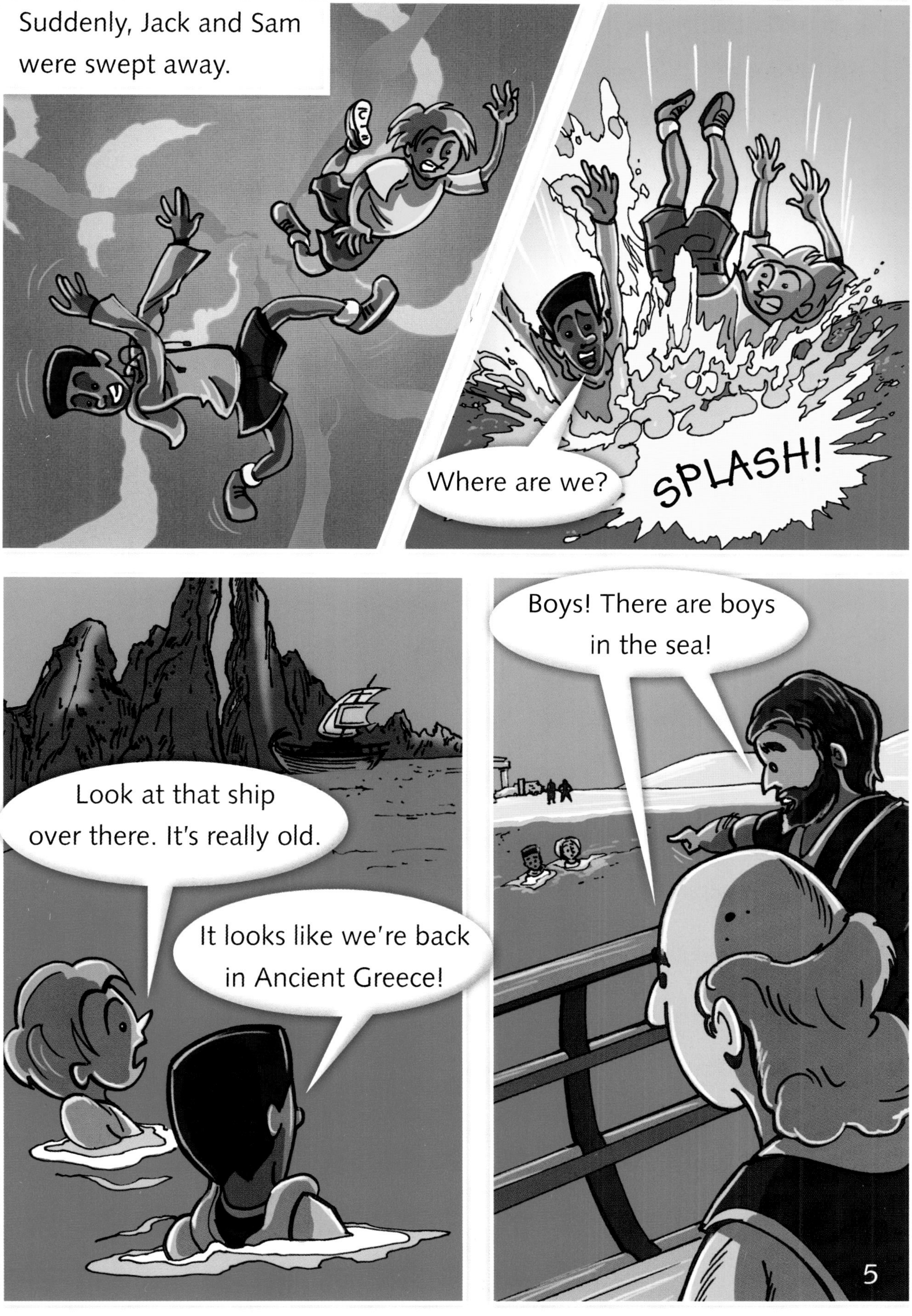
Suddenly, Jack and Sam were swept away.
Where are we?
SPLASH!
Look at that ship over there. It's really old.
It looks like we're back in Ancient Greece!
Boys! There are boys in the sea!

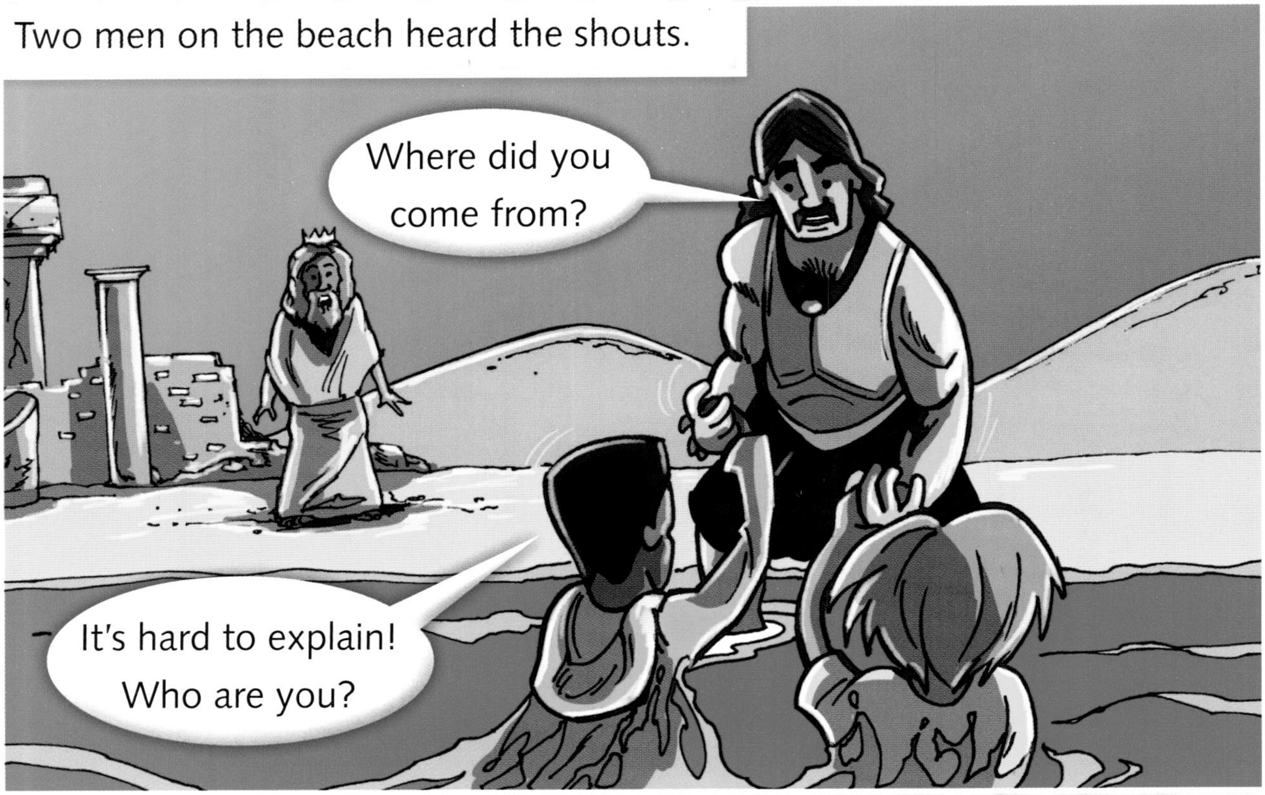
Two men on the beach heard the shouts.
Where did you come from?
It's hard to explain! Who are you?

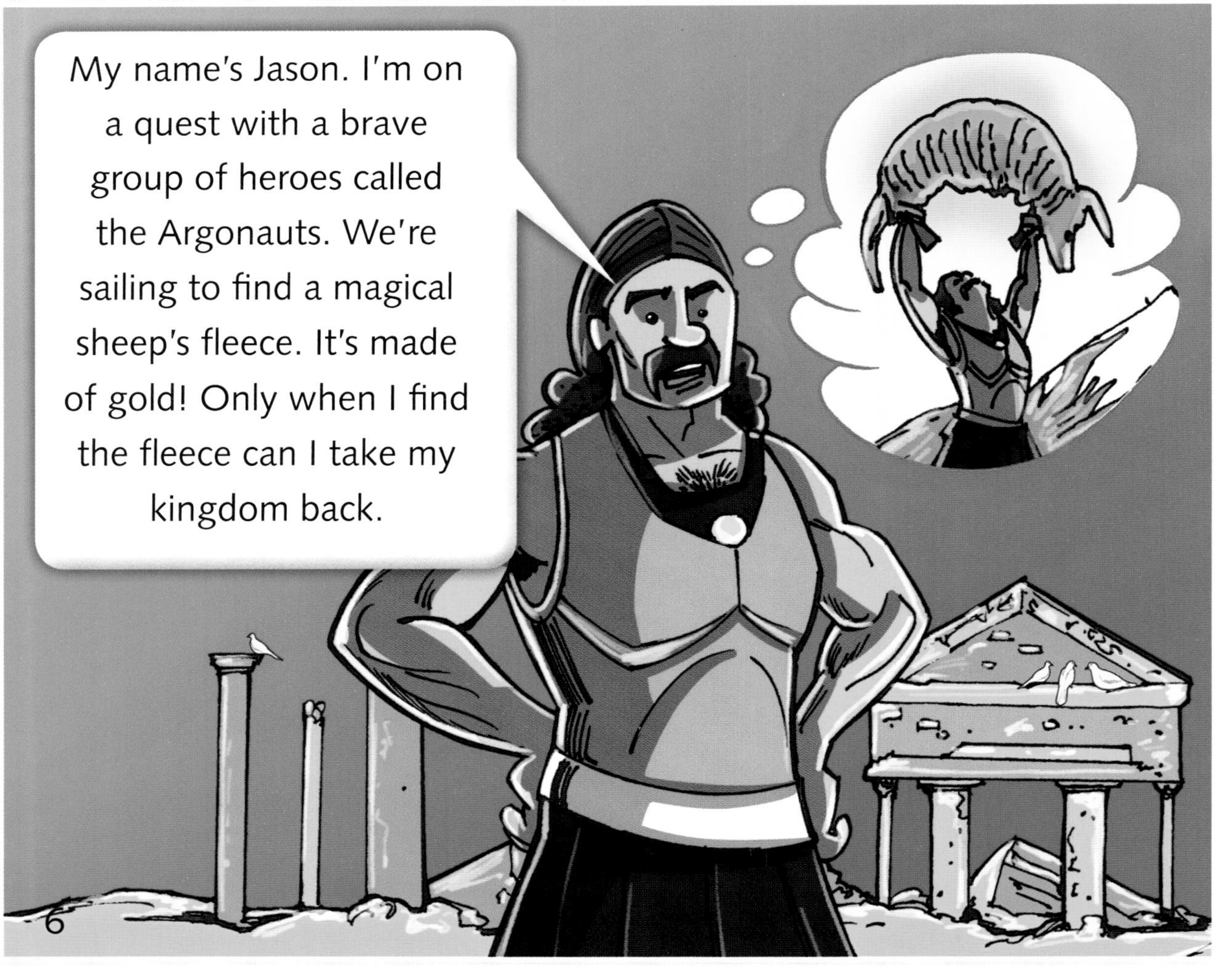
My name's Jason. I'm on a quest with a brave group of heroes called the Argonauts. We're sailing to find a magical sheep's fleece. It's made of gold! Only when I find the fleece can I take my kingdom back.

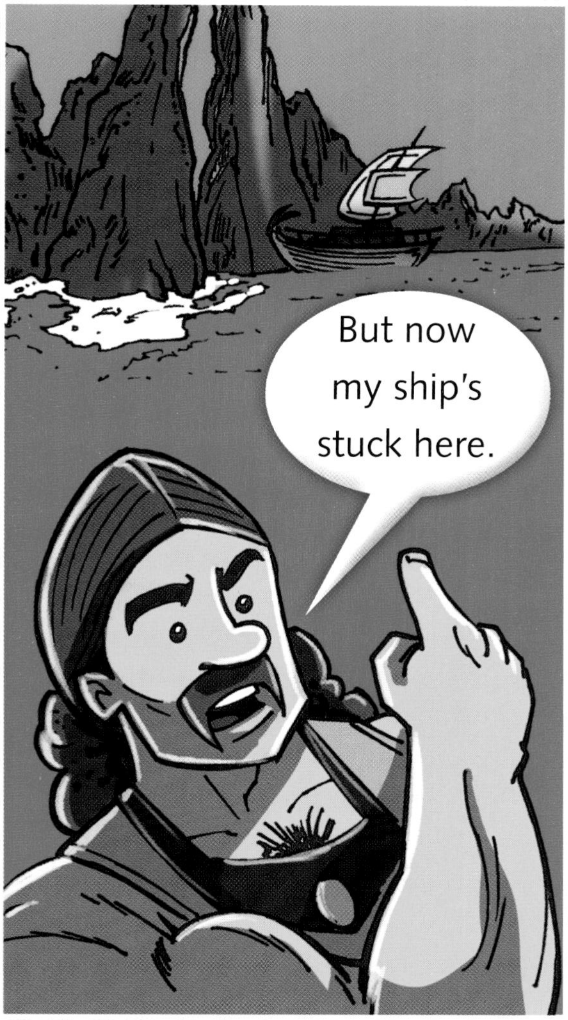
But now my ship's stuck here.

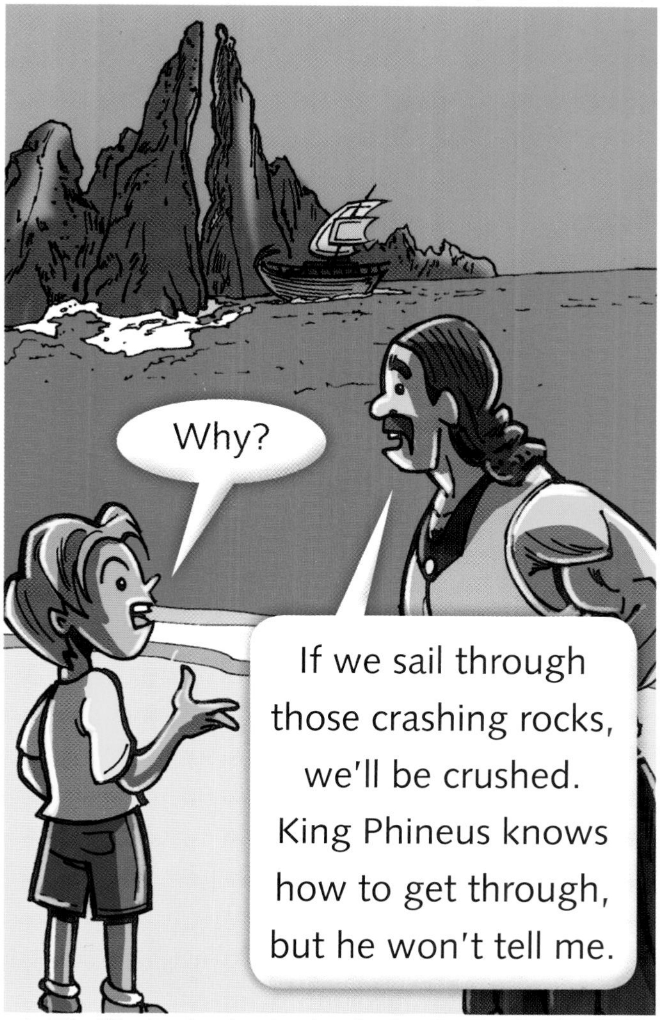
Why?
If we sail through those crashing rocks, we'll be crushed. King Phineus knows how to get through, but he won't tell me.

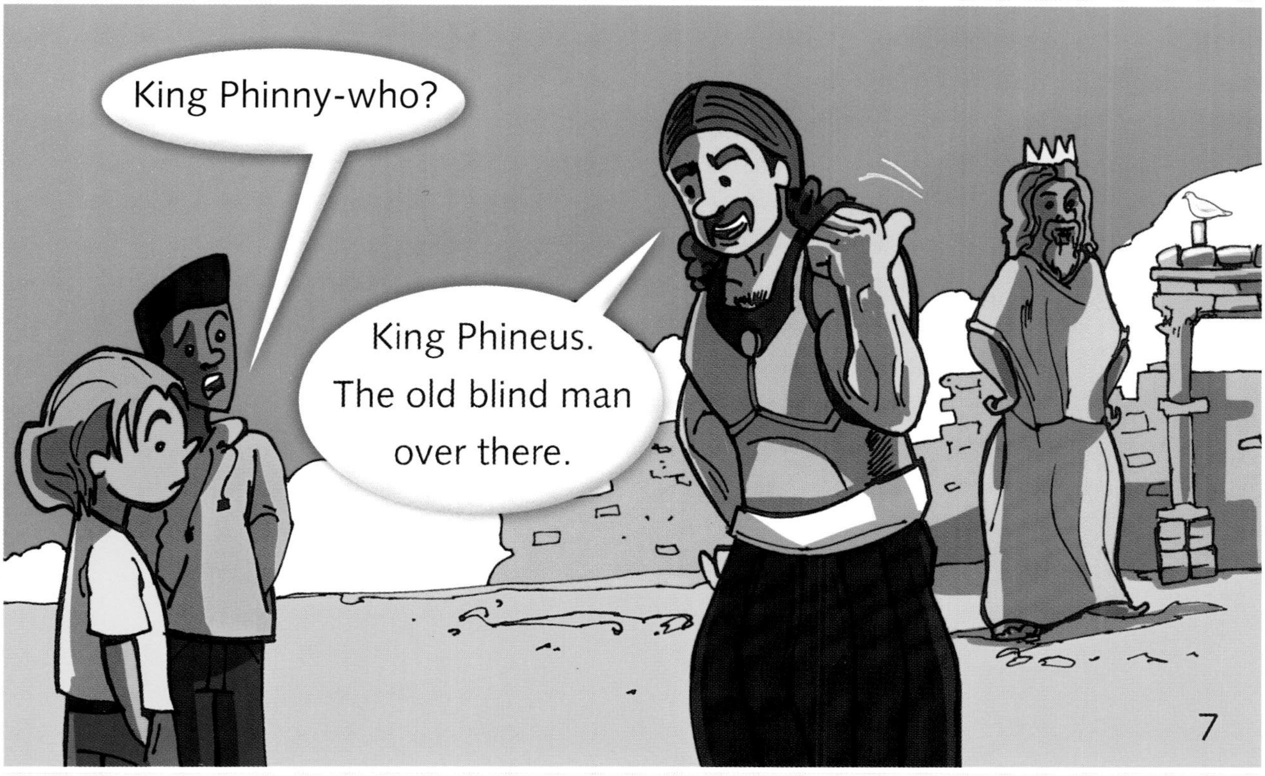
King Phinny-who?
King Phineus. The old blind man over there.

Jason explained that a god was punishing King Phineus. Every day, food appeared on the table but Harpies attacked before he could eat it.

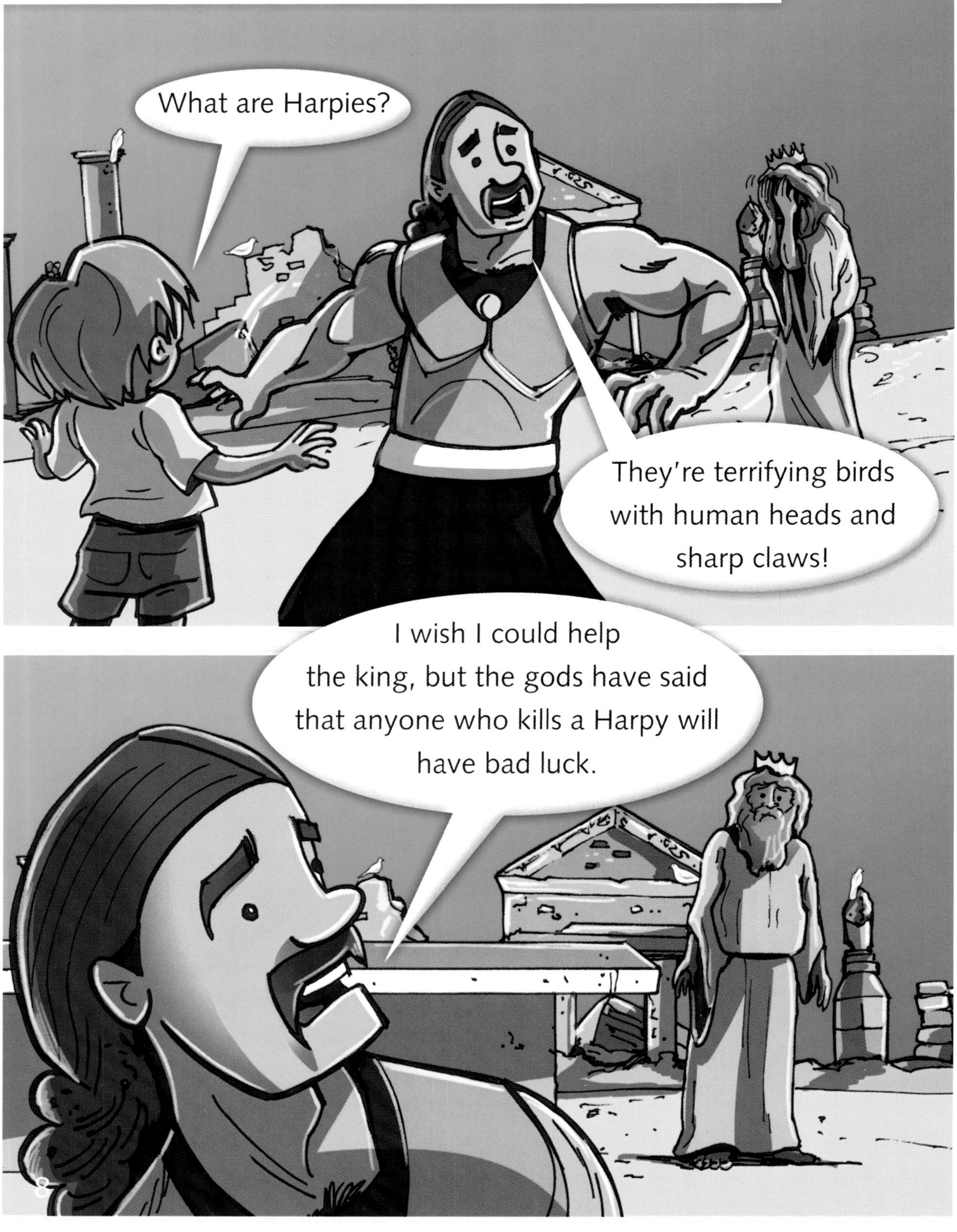
What are Harpies?
They're terrifying birds with human heads and sharp claws!
I wish I could help the king, but the gods have said that anyone who kills a Harpy will have bad luck.

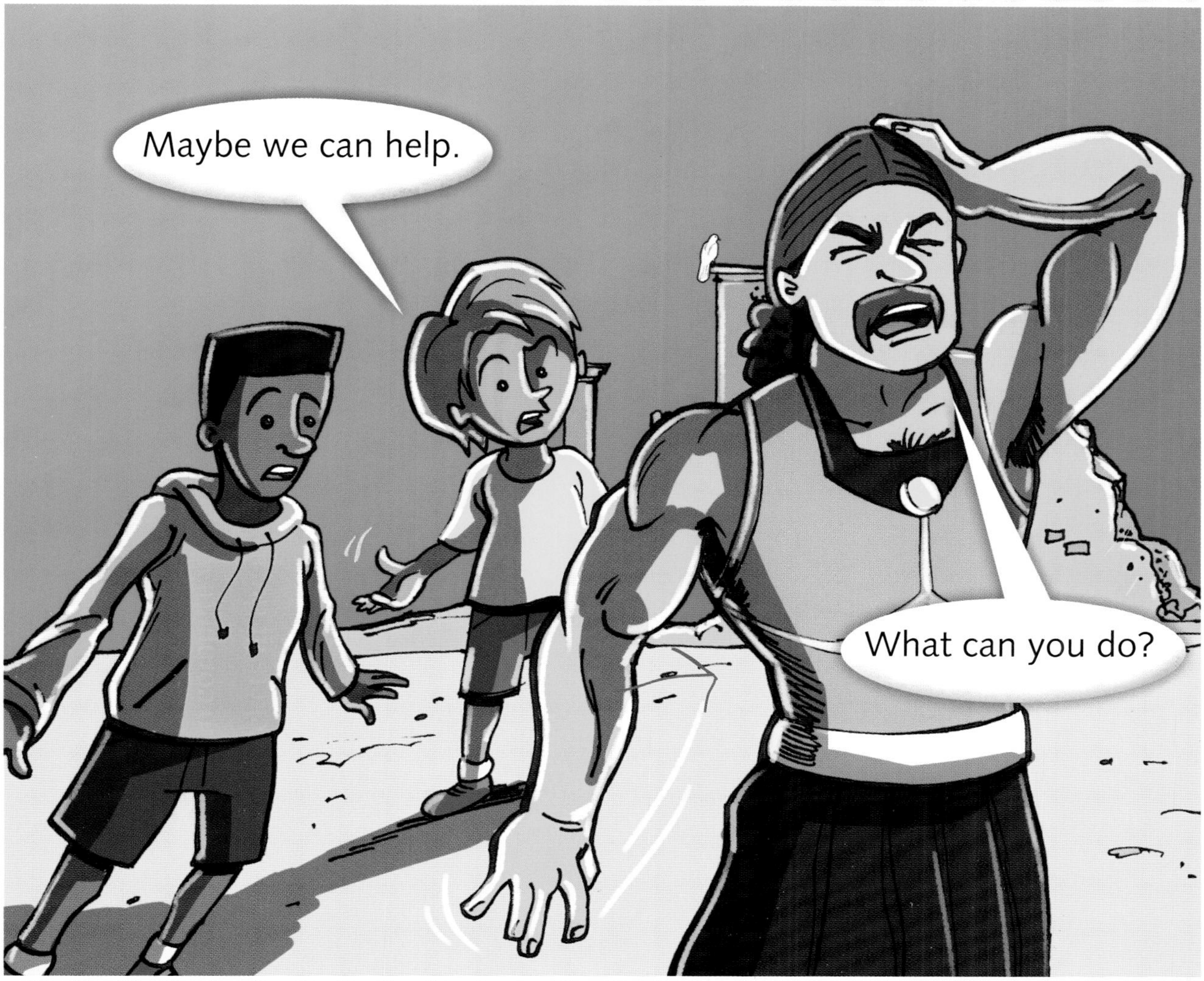
Maybe we can help.
What can you do?

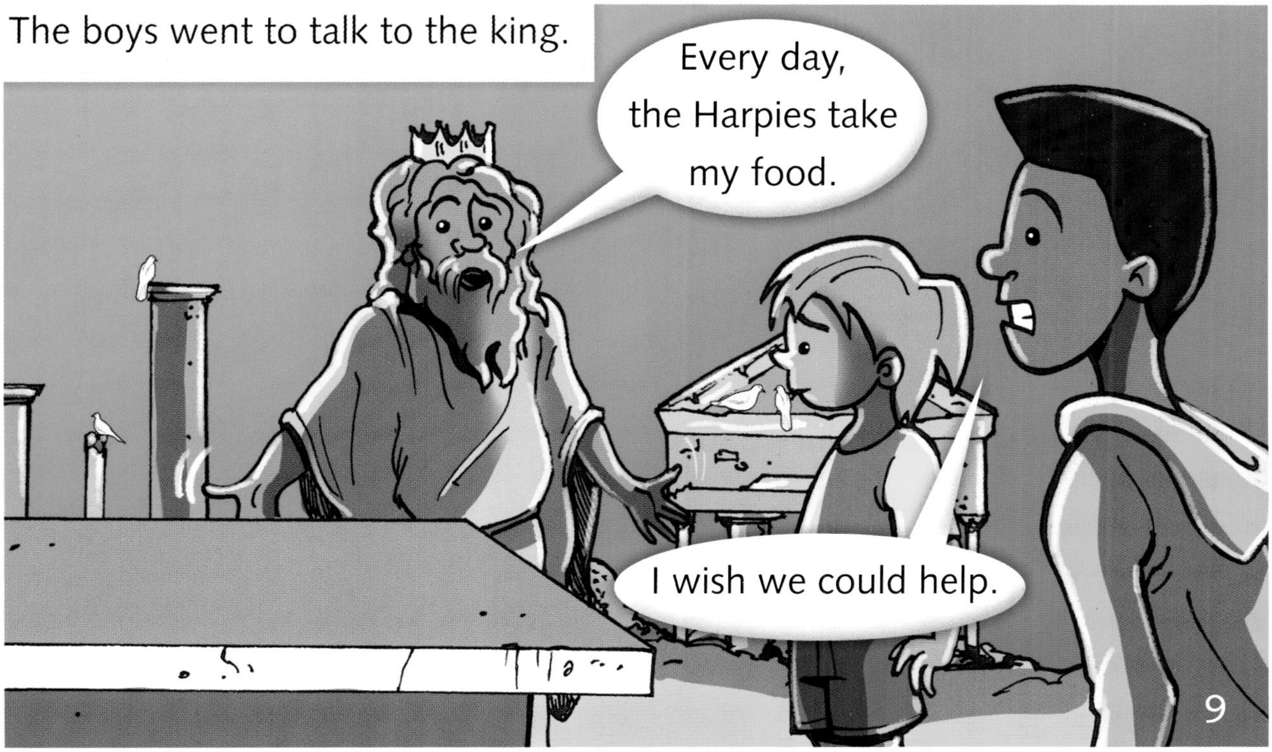
The boys went to talk to the king.
Every day, the Harpies take my food.
I wish we could help.

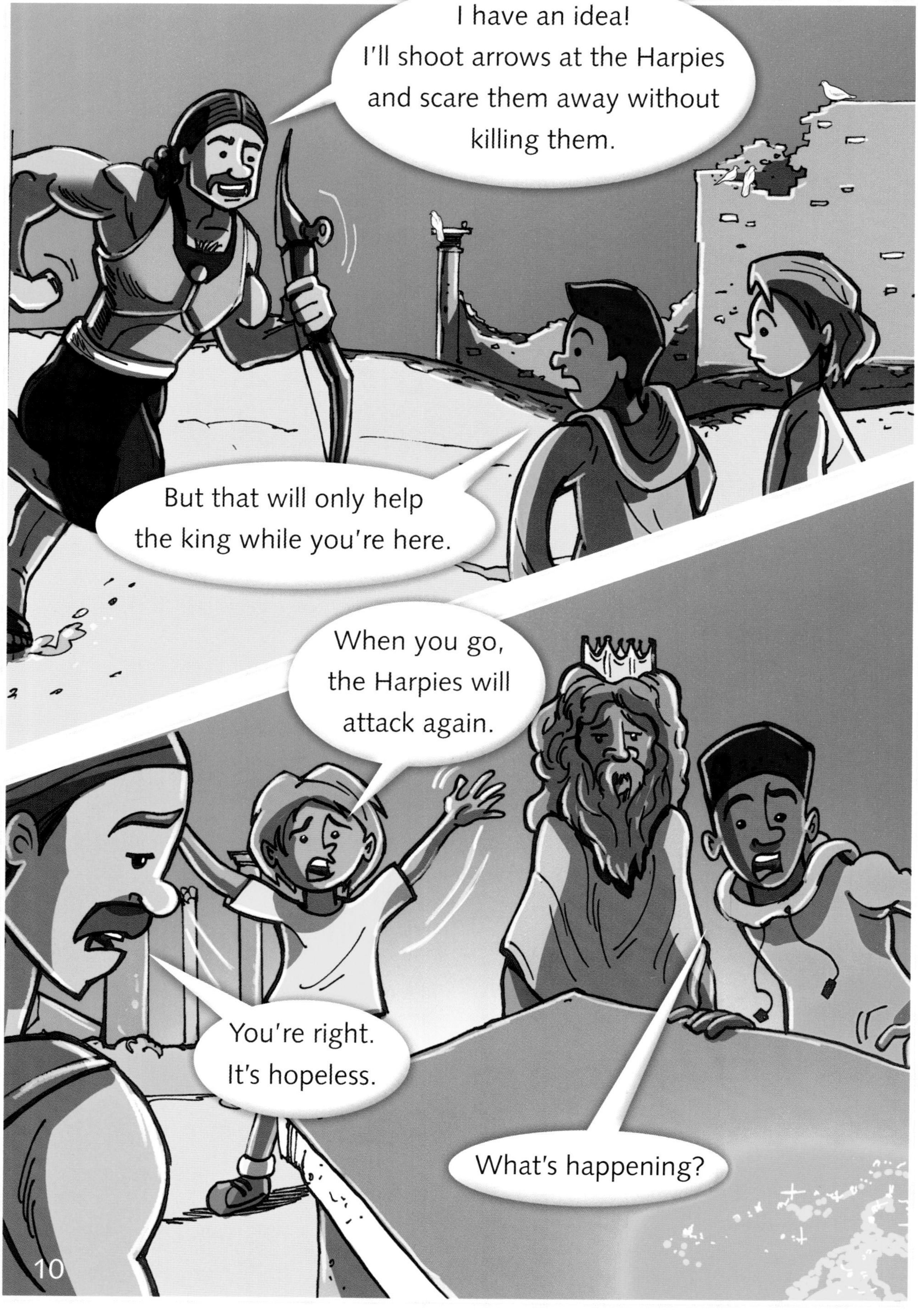
I have an idea!
I'll shoot arrows at the Harpies and scare them away without killing them.
But that will only help the king while you're here.
When you go, the Harpies will attack again.
You're right. It's hopeless.
What's happening?

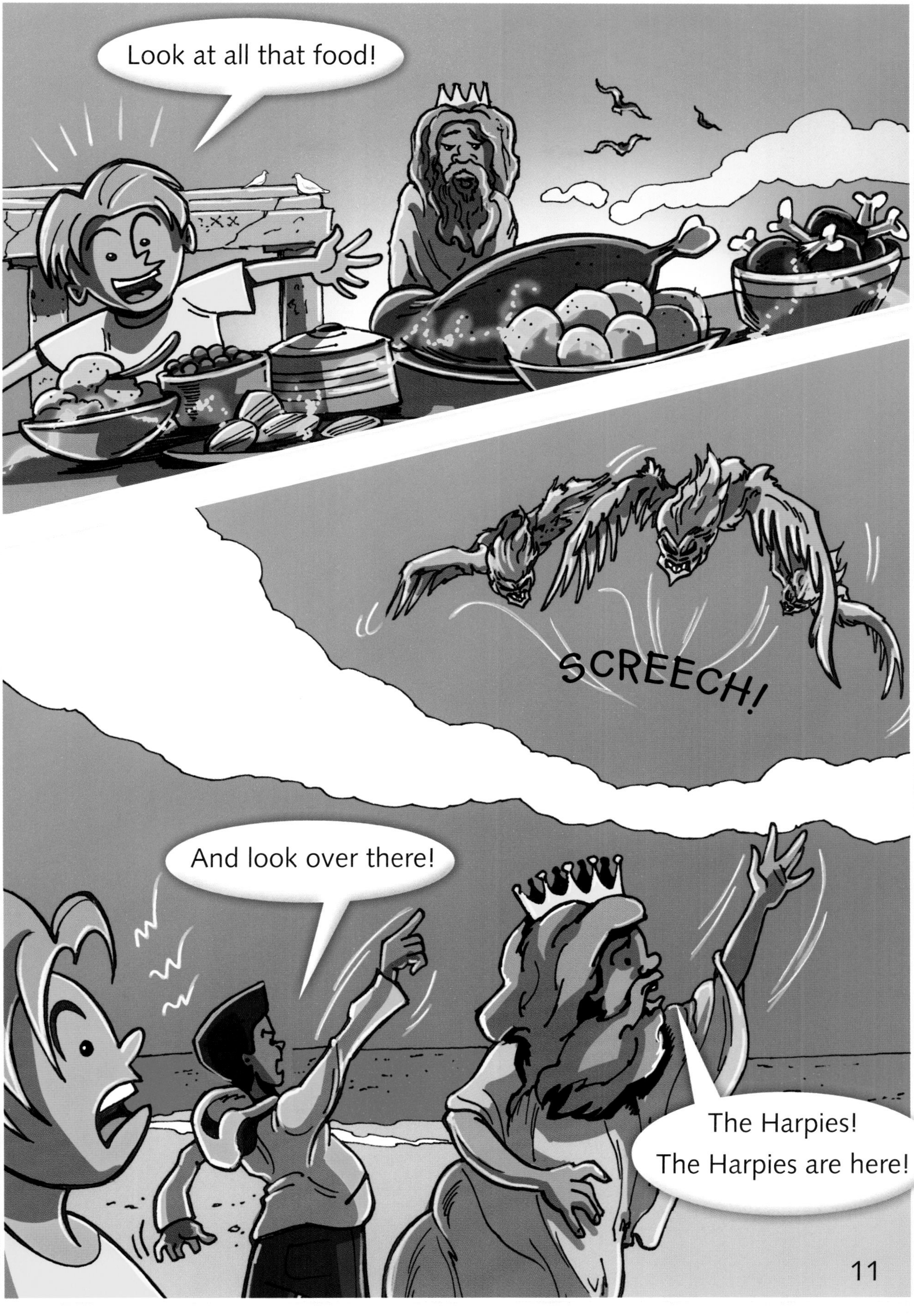
Look at all that food!
SCREECH!
And look over there!
The Harpies! The Harpies are here!

The Harpies attacked.

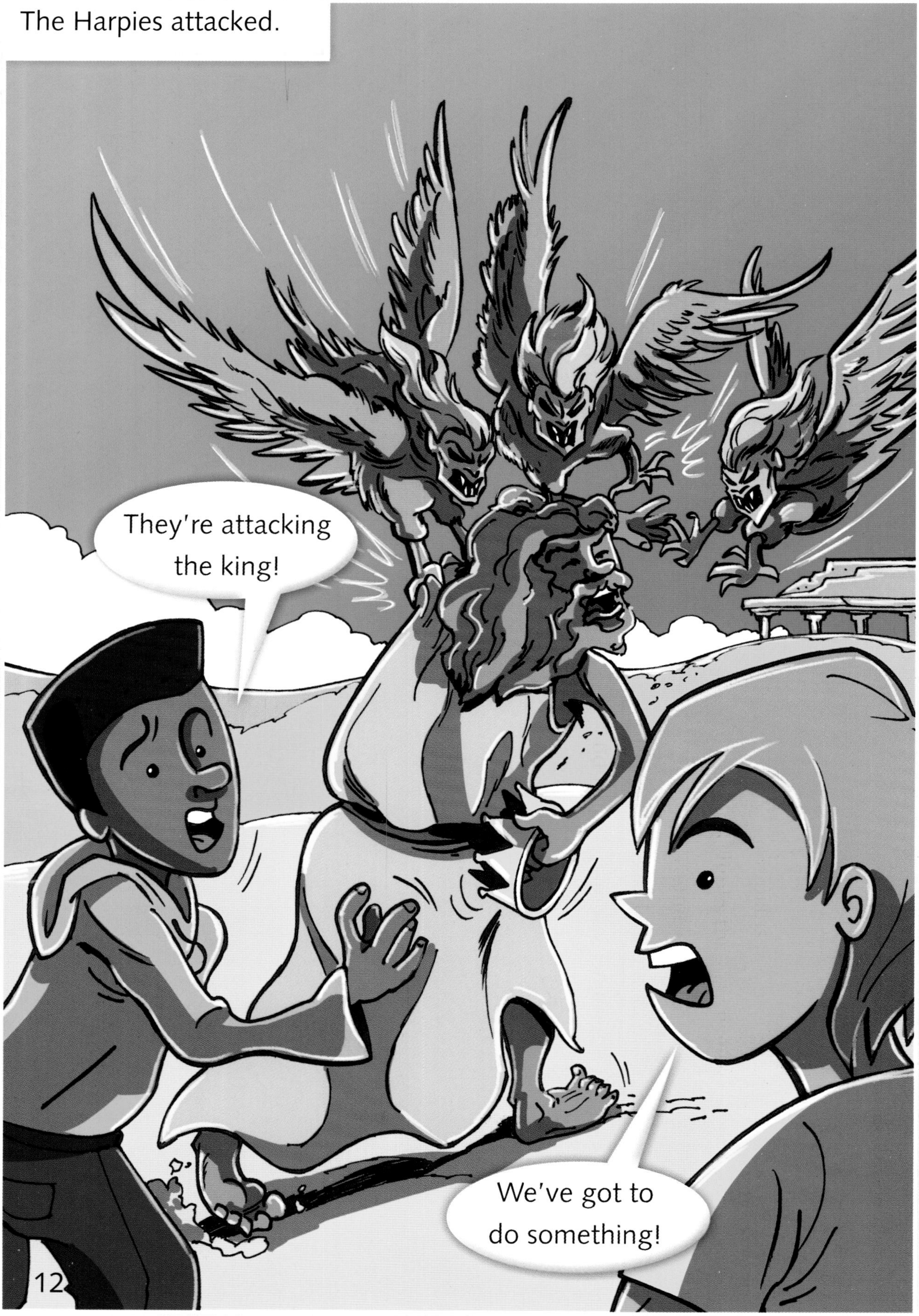
They're attacking the king!
We've got to do something!

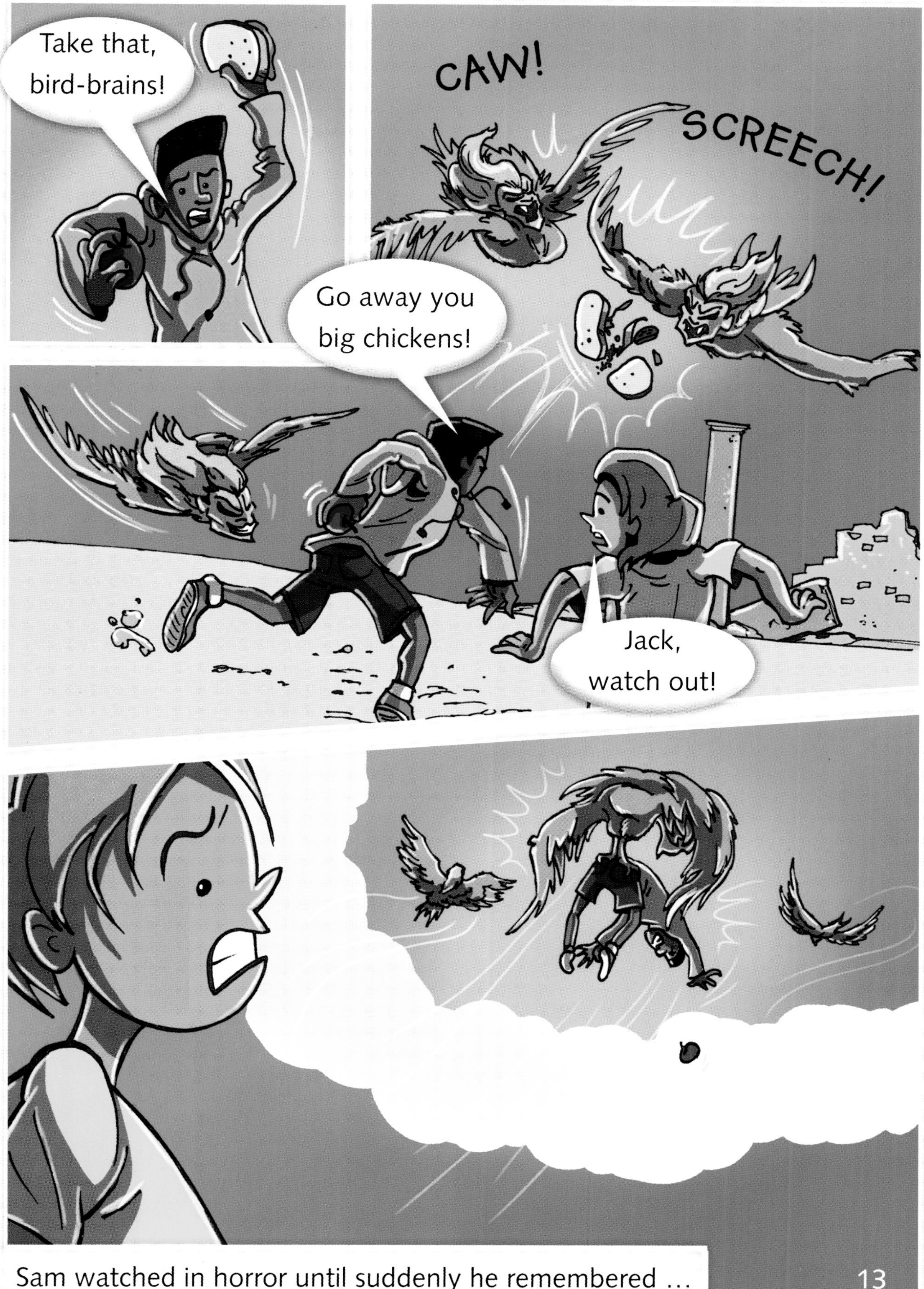
Take that, bird-brains!
CAW!
SCREECH!
Go away you big chickens!
Jack, watch out!

Sam watched in horror until suddenly he remembered …

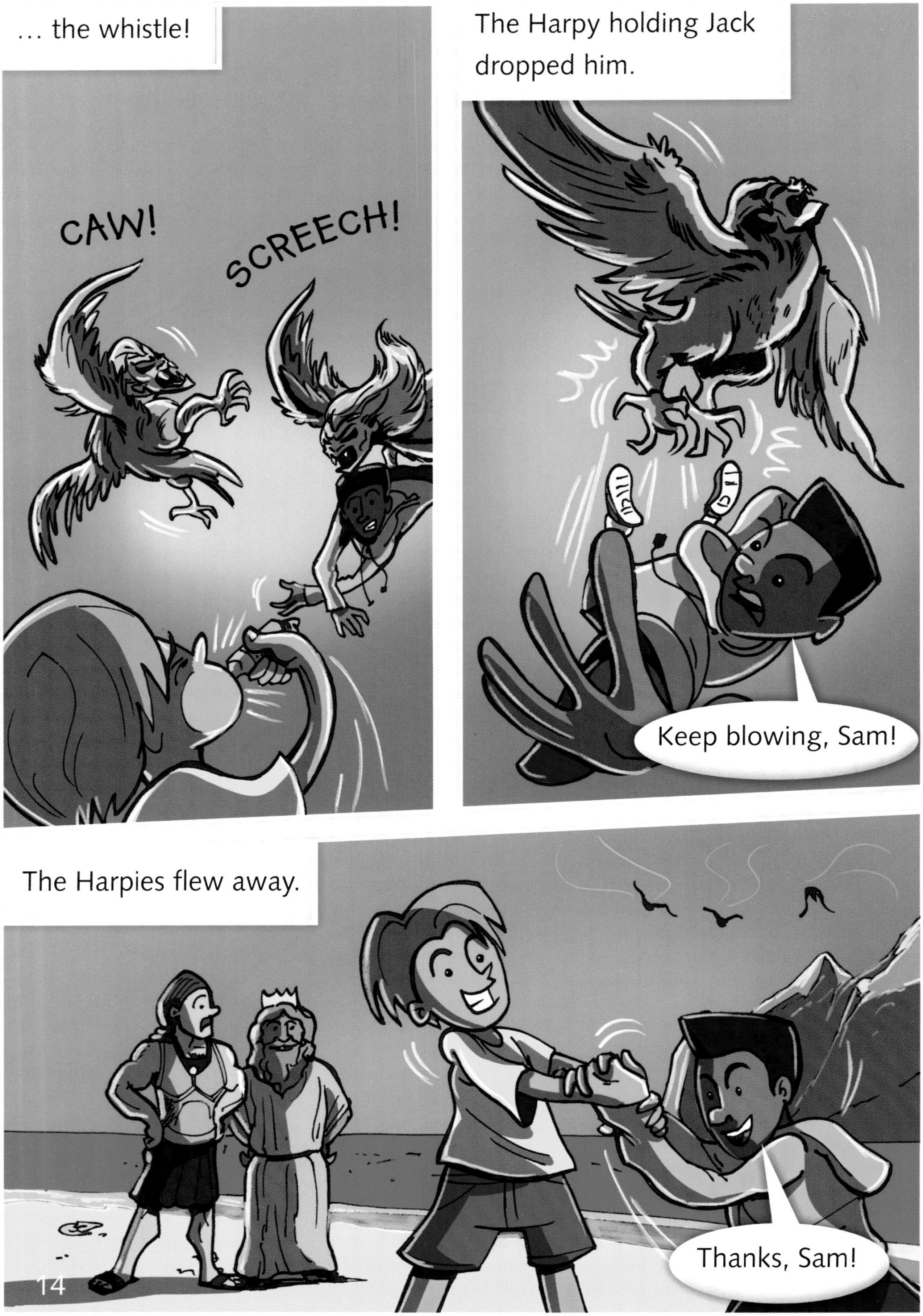
… the whistle!
CAW!
SCREECH!
The Harpy holding Jack dropped him.
Keep blowing, Sam!
The Harpies flew away.
Thanks, Sam!

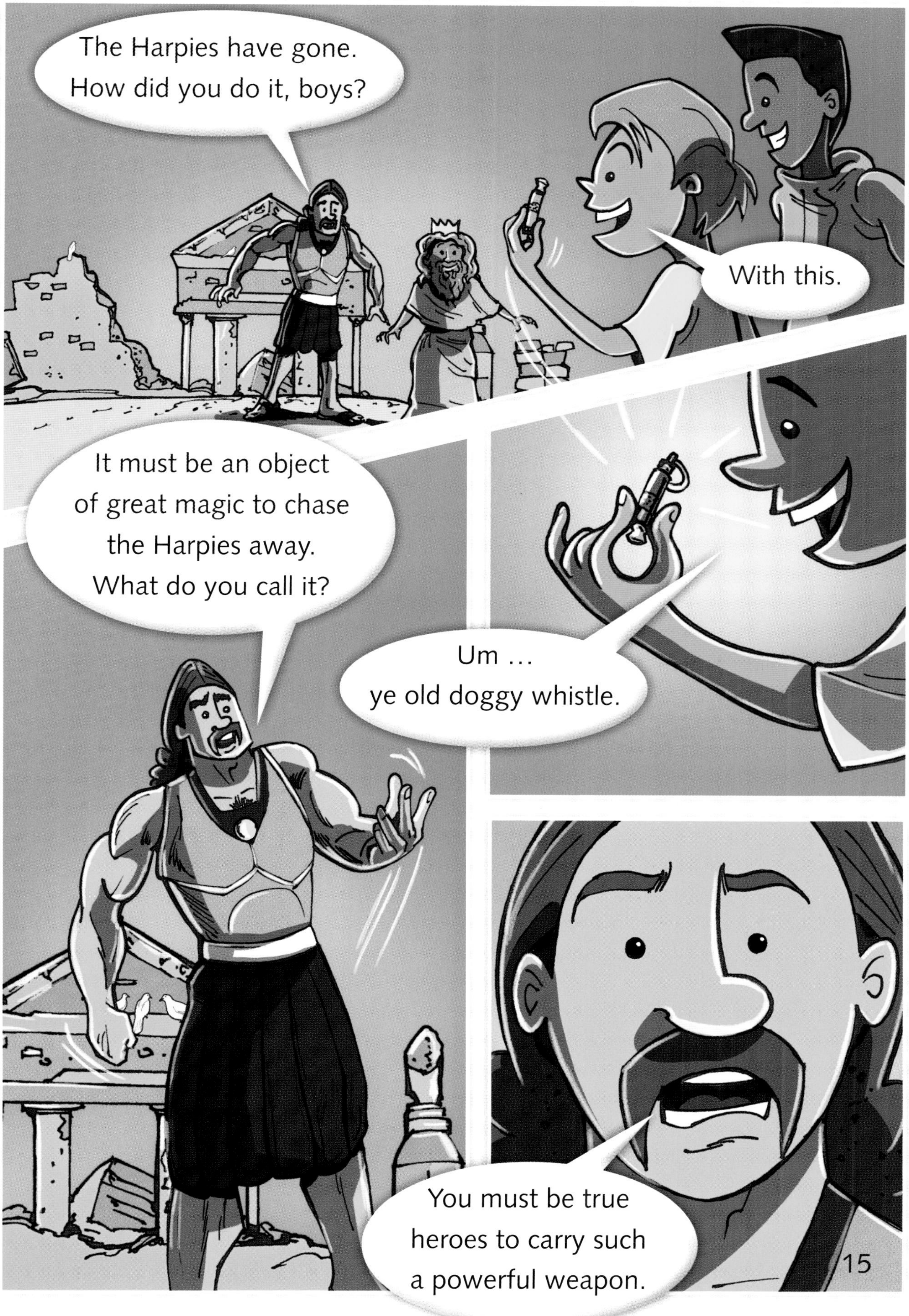

The Harpies have gone. How did you do it, boys?
With this.
It must be an object of great magic to chase the Harpies away. What do you call it?
Um … ye old doggy whistle.
You must be true heroes to carry such a powerful weapon.

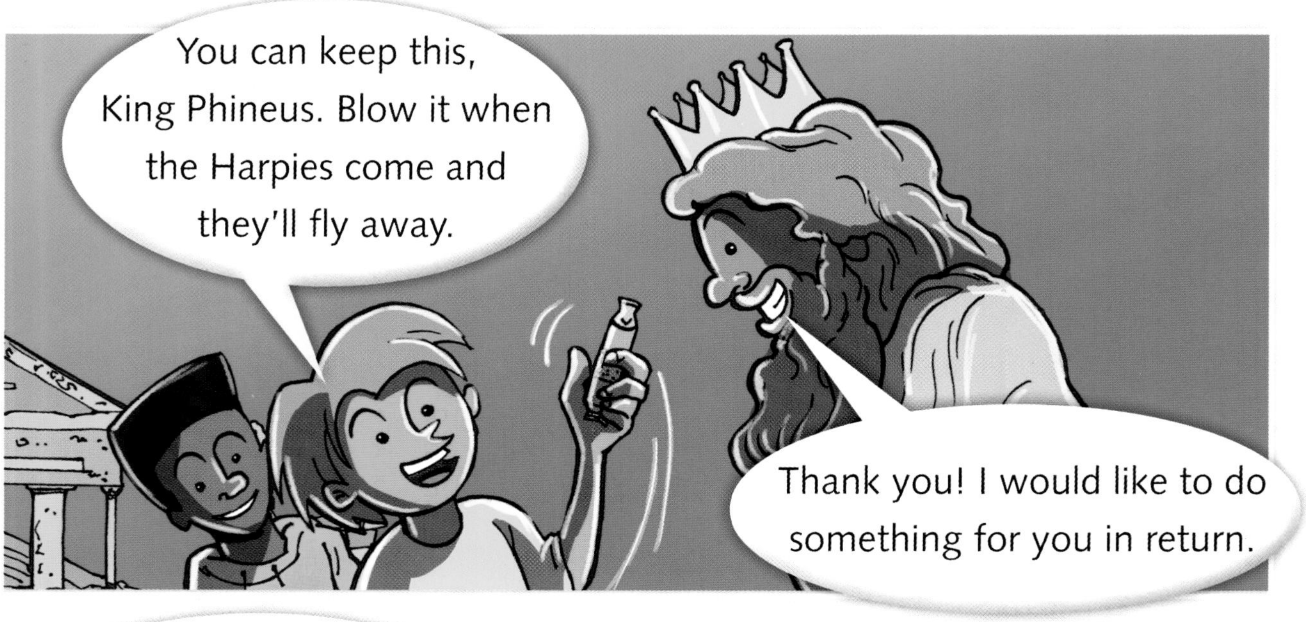
You can keep this, King Phineus. Blow it when the Harpies come and they'll fly away.
Thank you! I would like to do something for you in return.

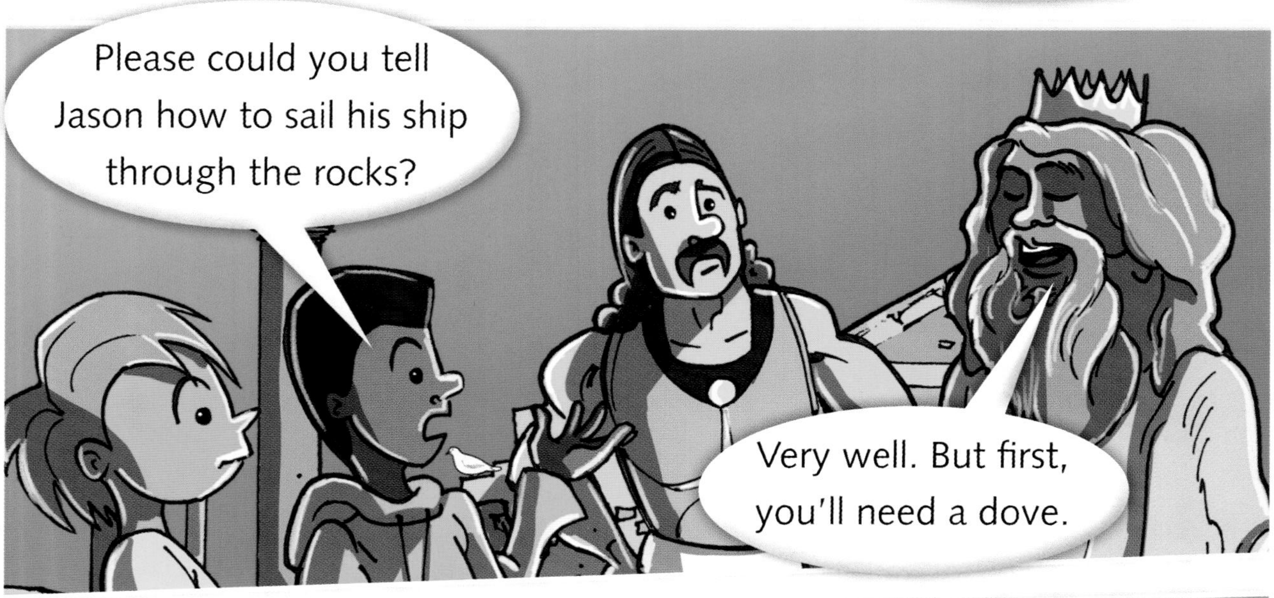
Please could you tell Jason how to sail his ship through the rocks?
Very well. But first, you'll need a dove.

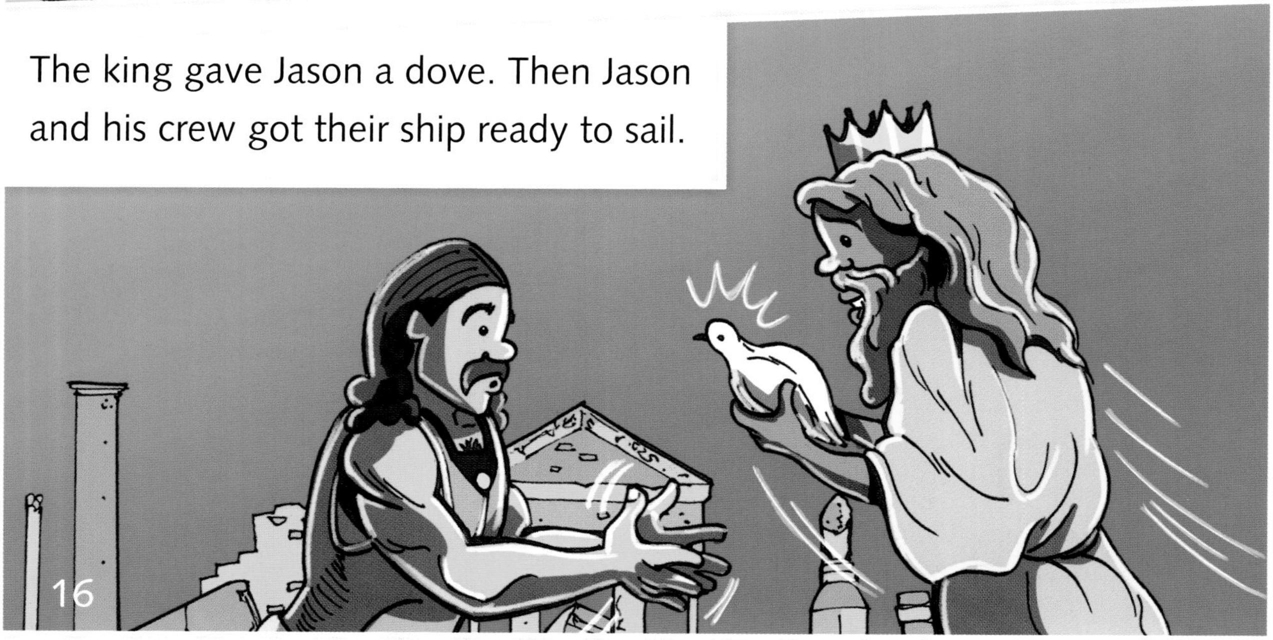
The king gave Jason a dove. Then Jason and his crew got their ship ready to sail.

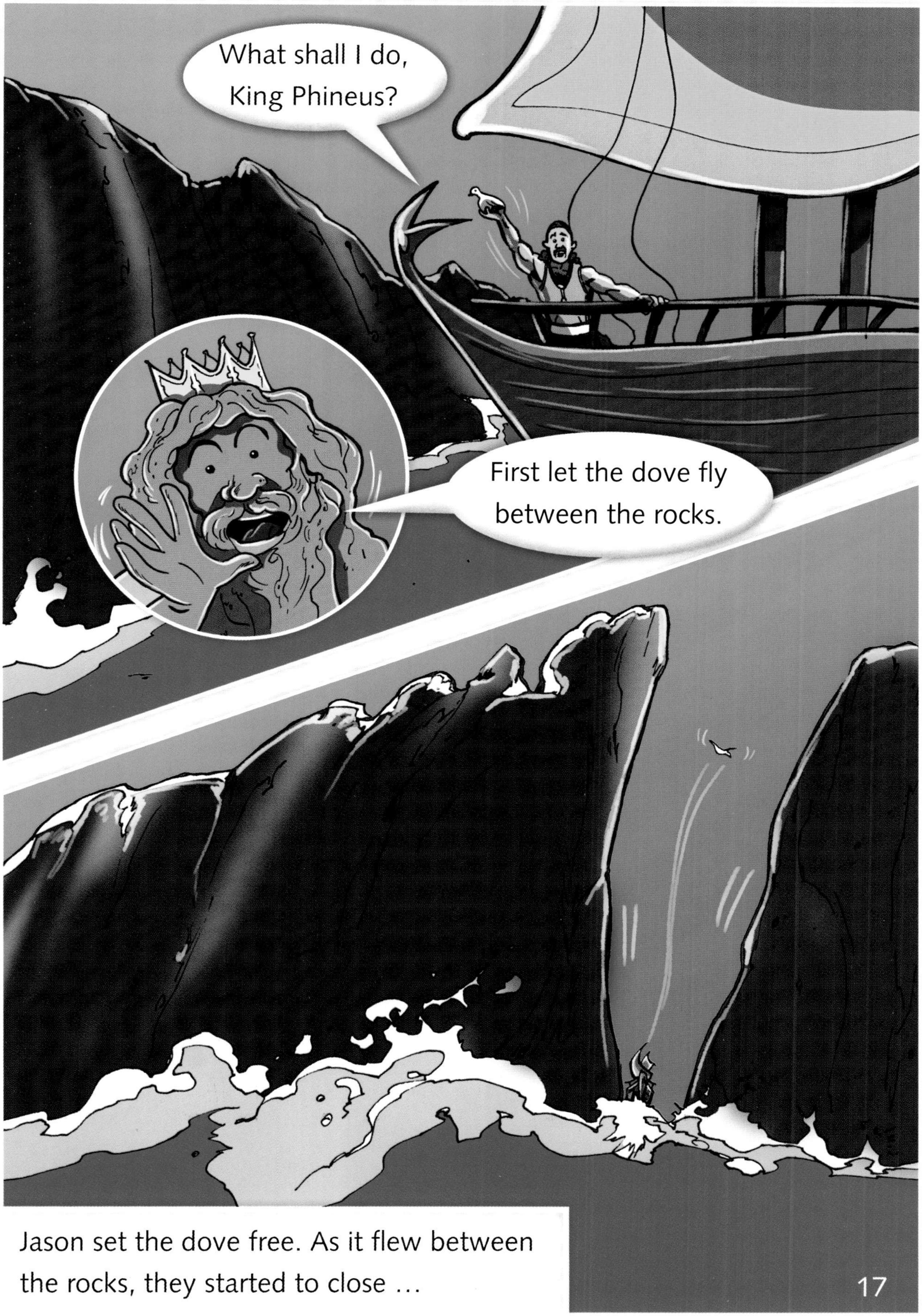
What shall I do, King Phineus?
First let the dove fly between the rocks.

Jason set the dove free. As it flew between the rocks, they started to close …

But the dove flew so fast, it only lost one feather.

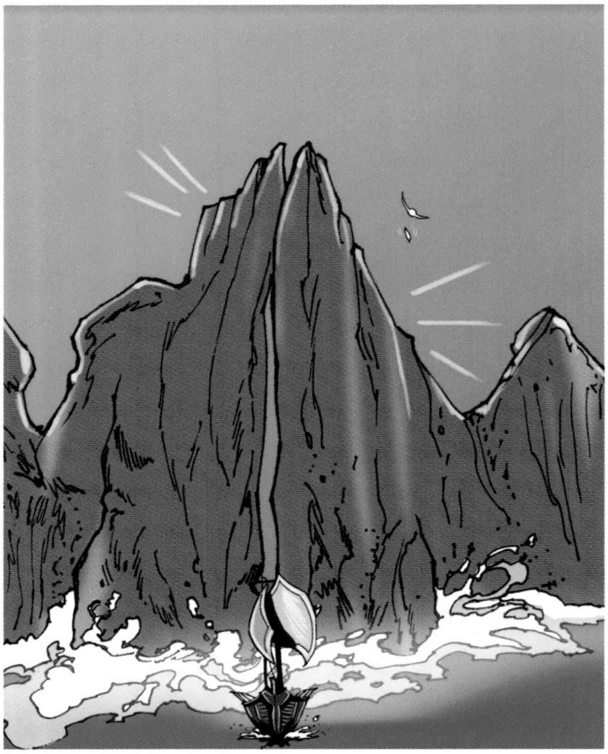

The rocks started to move apart again.

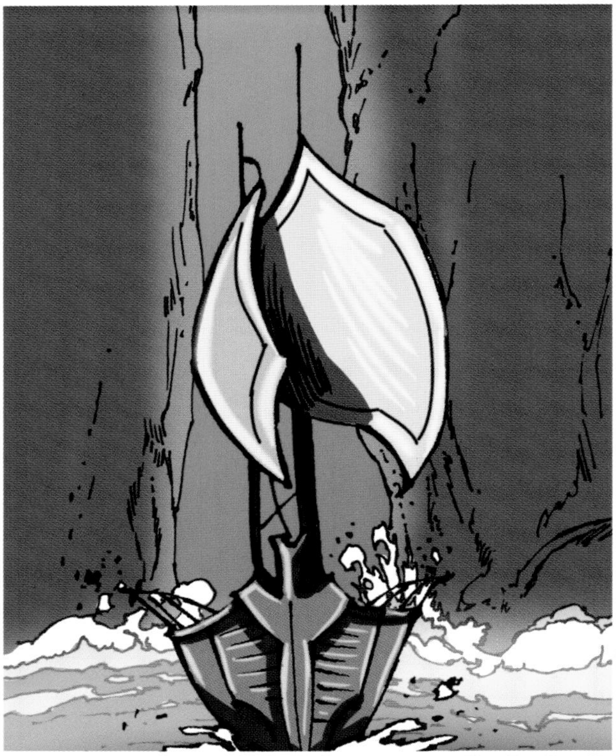

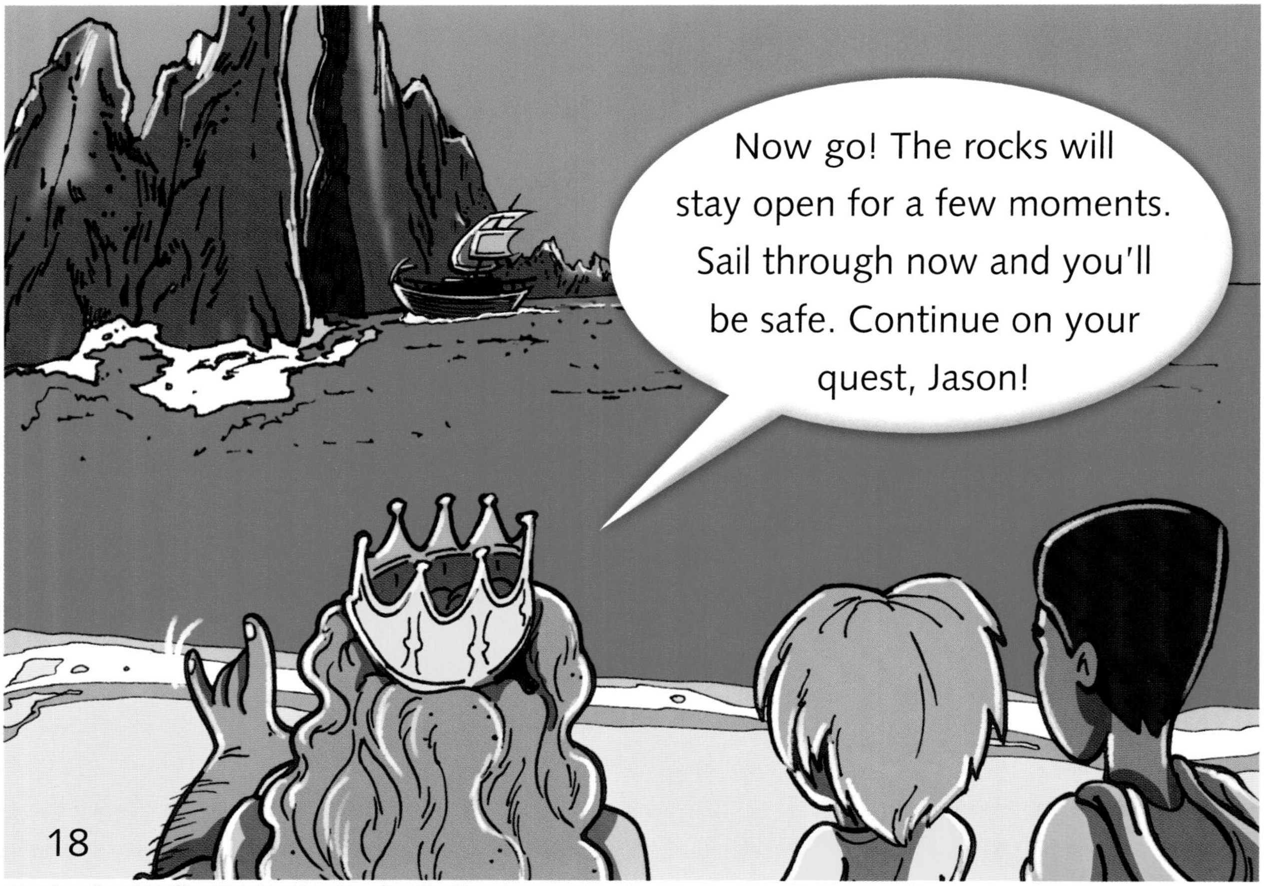
Now go! The rocks will stay open for a few moments. Sail through now and you'll be safe. Continue on your quest, Jason!

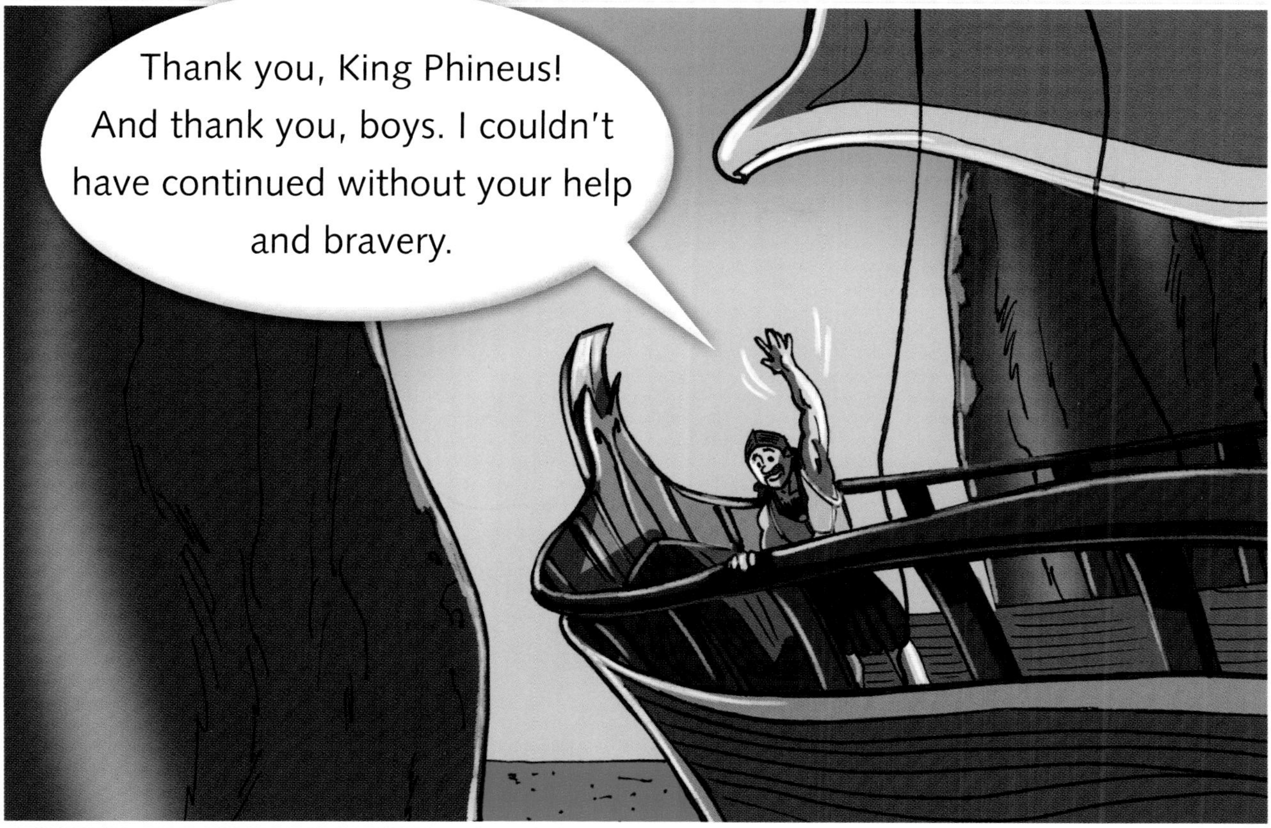
Thank you, King Phineus! And thank you, boys. I couldn't have continued without your help and bravery.

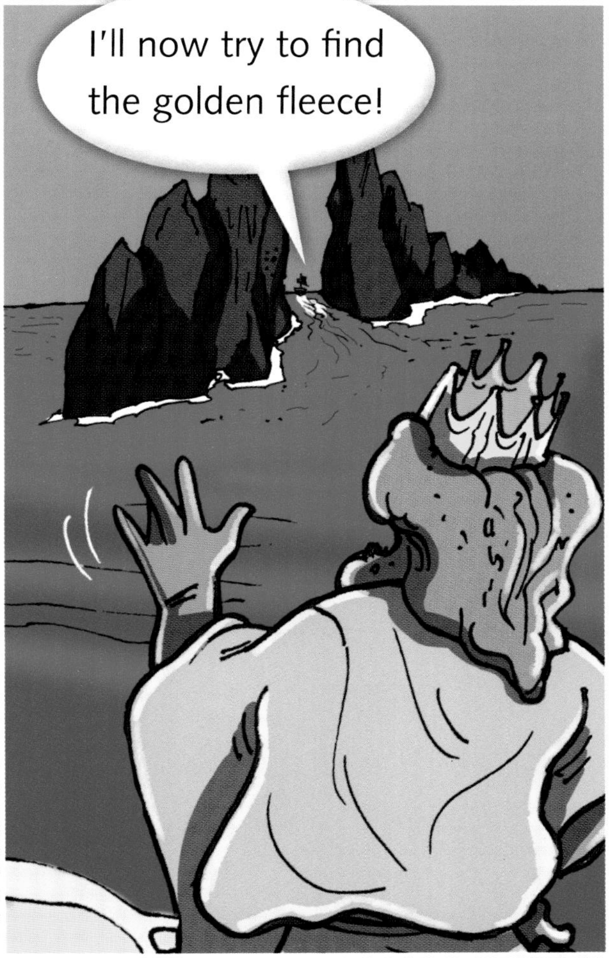
I'll now try to find the golden fleece!

Suddenly the spoon glowed.

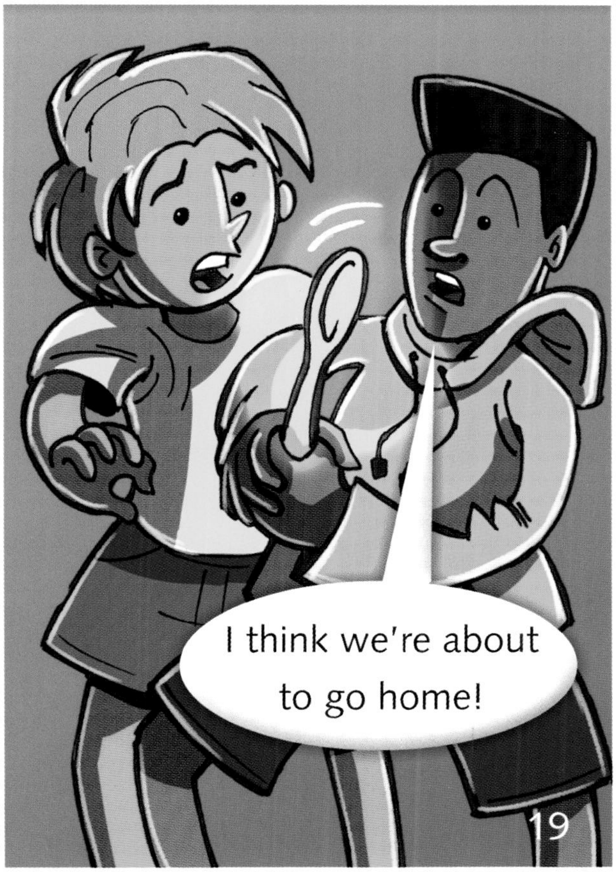
I think we're about to go home!

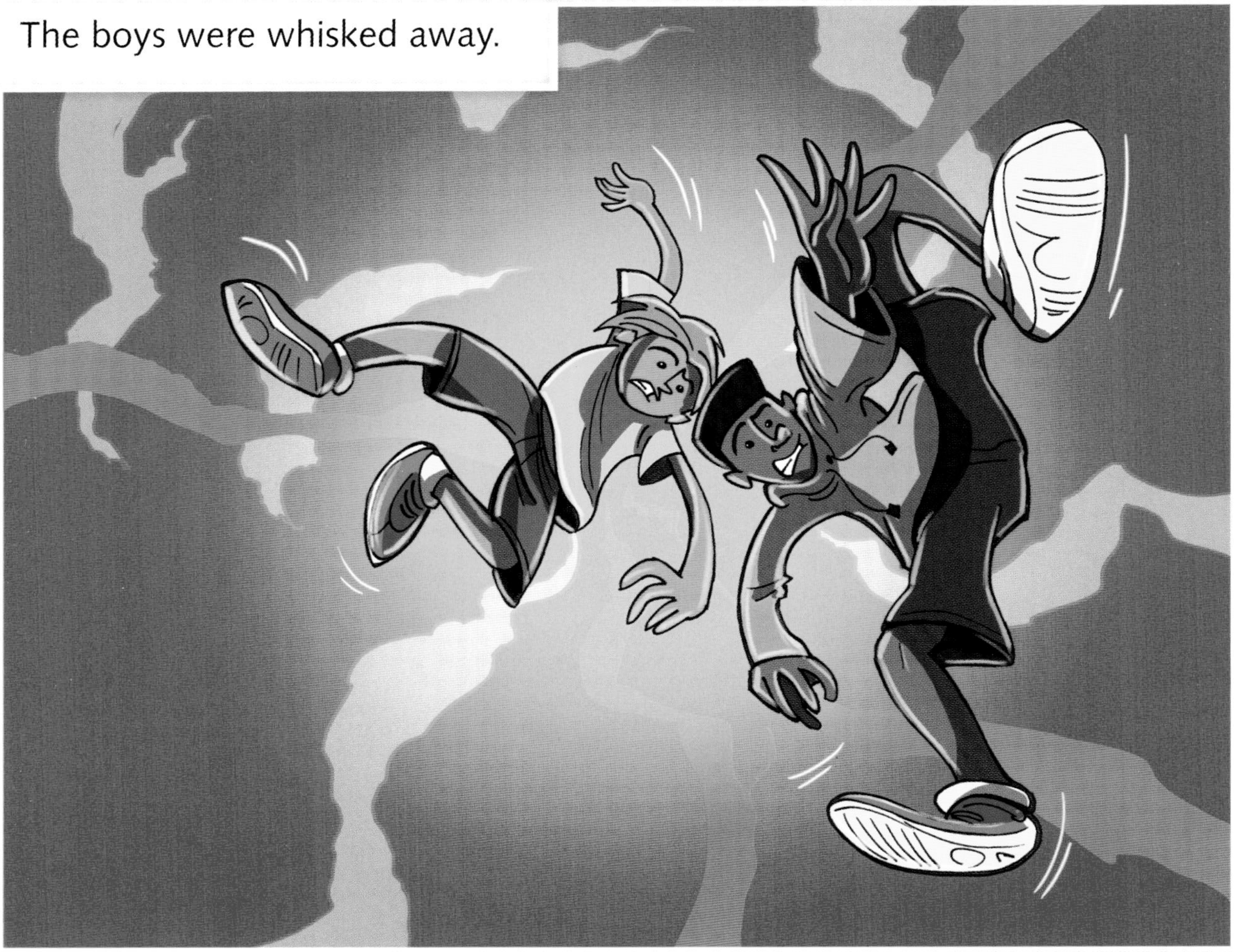
The boys were whisked away.

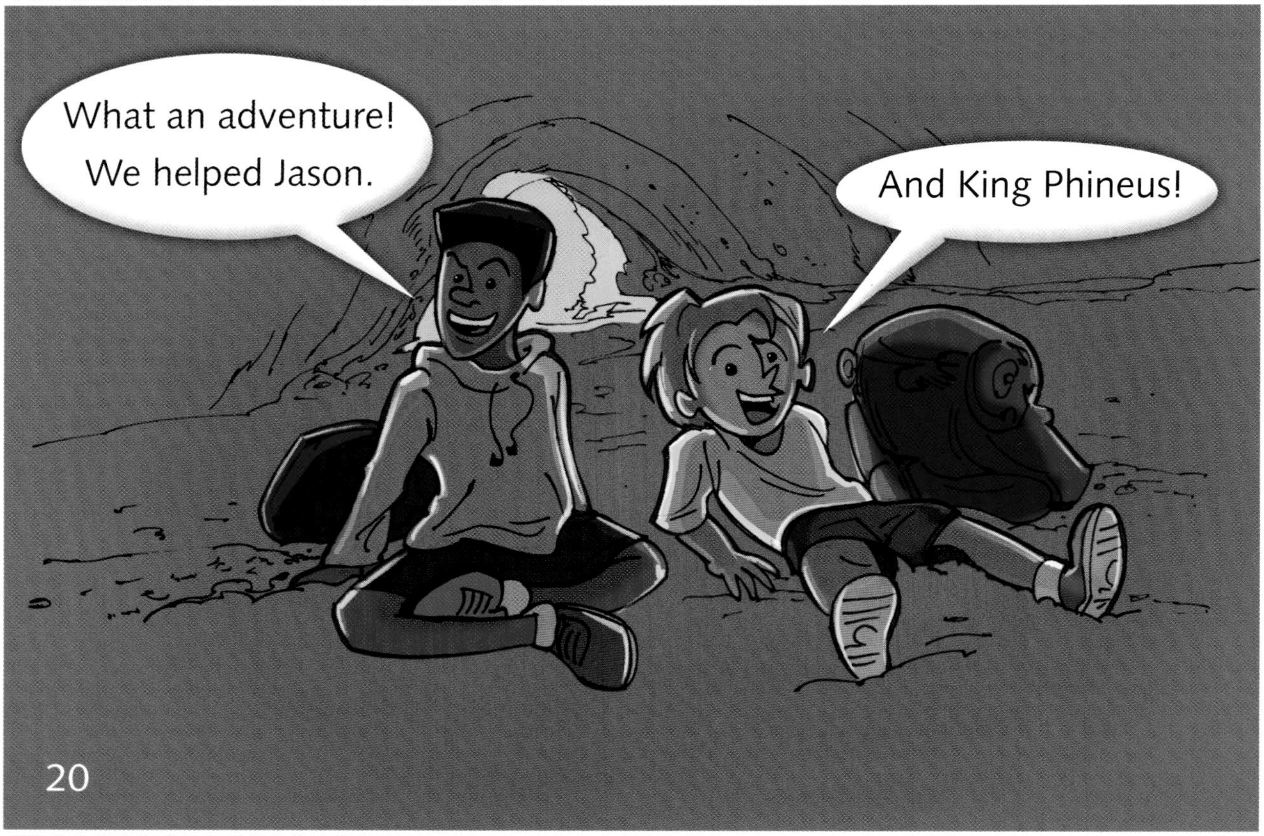
What an adventure! We helped Jason.
And King Phineus!

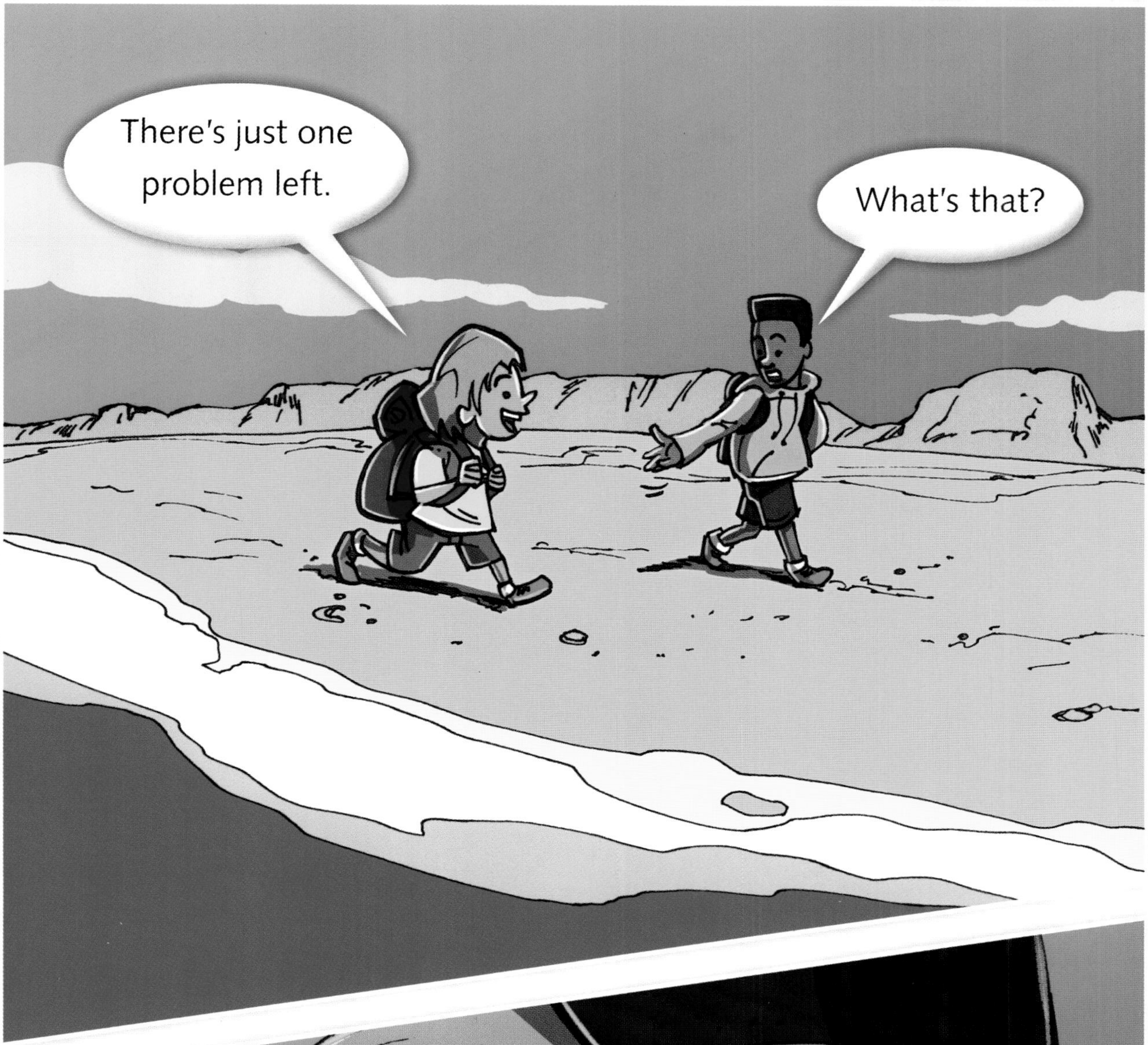
There's just one problem left.
What's that?

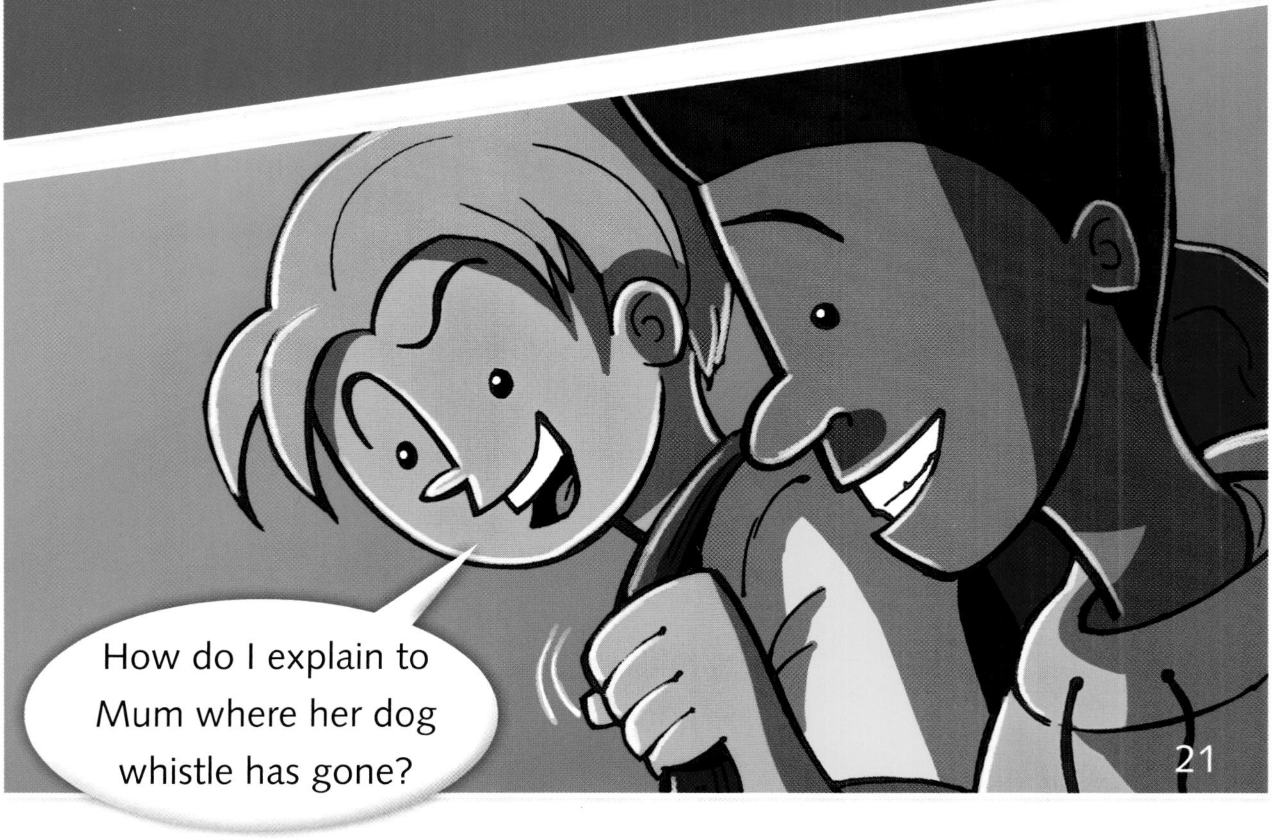
How do I explain to Mum where her dog whistle has gone?

Helping Jason

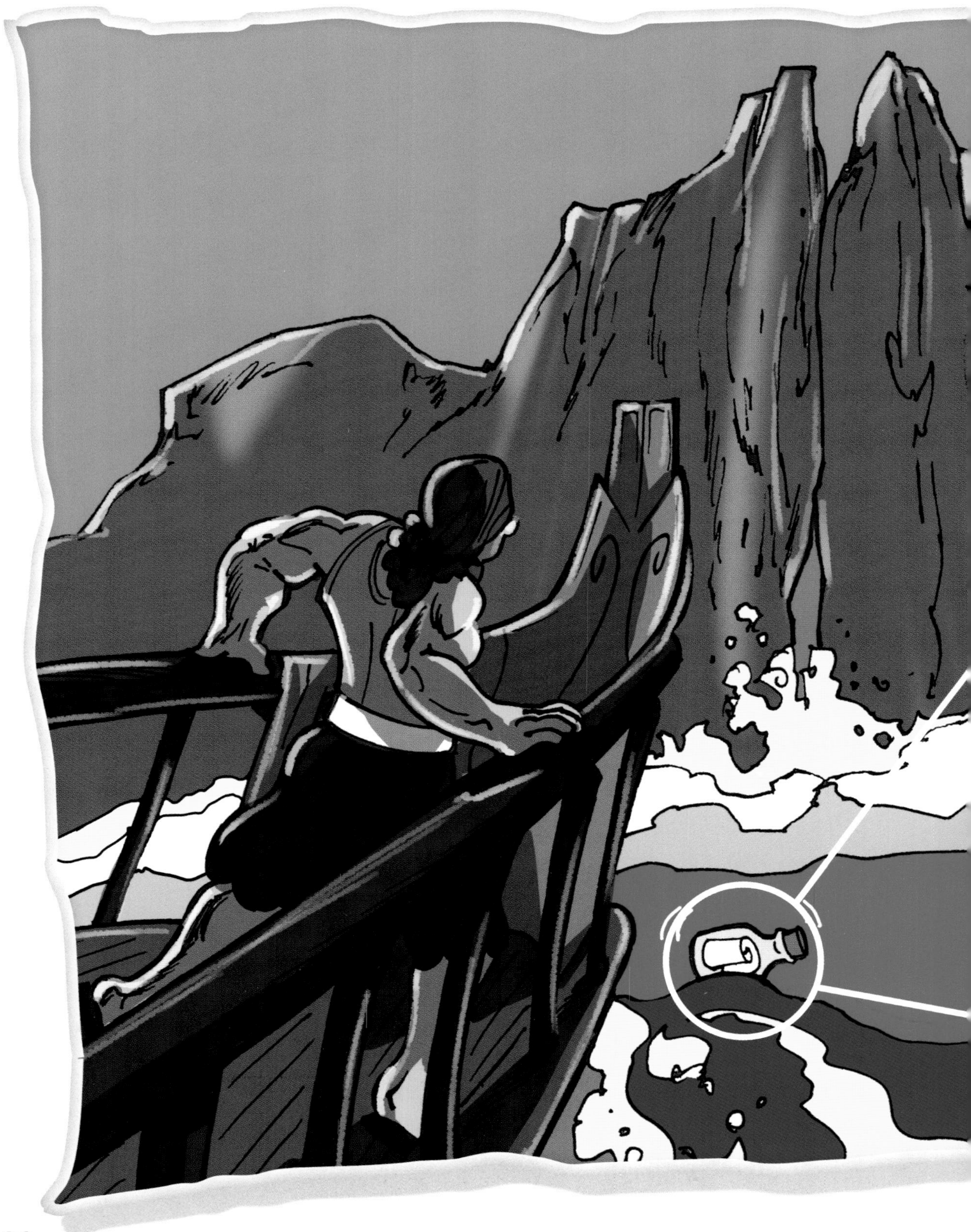

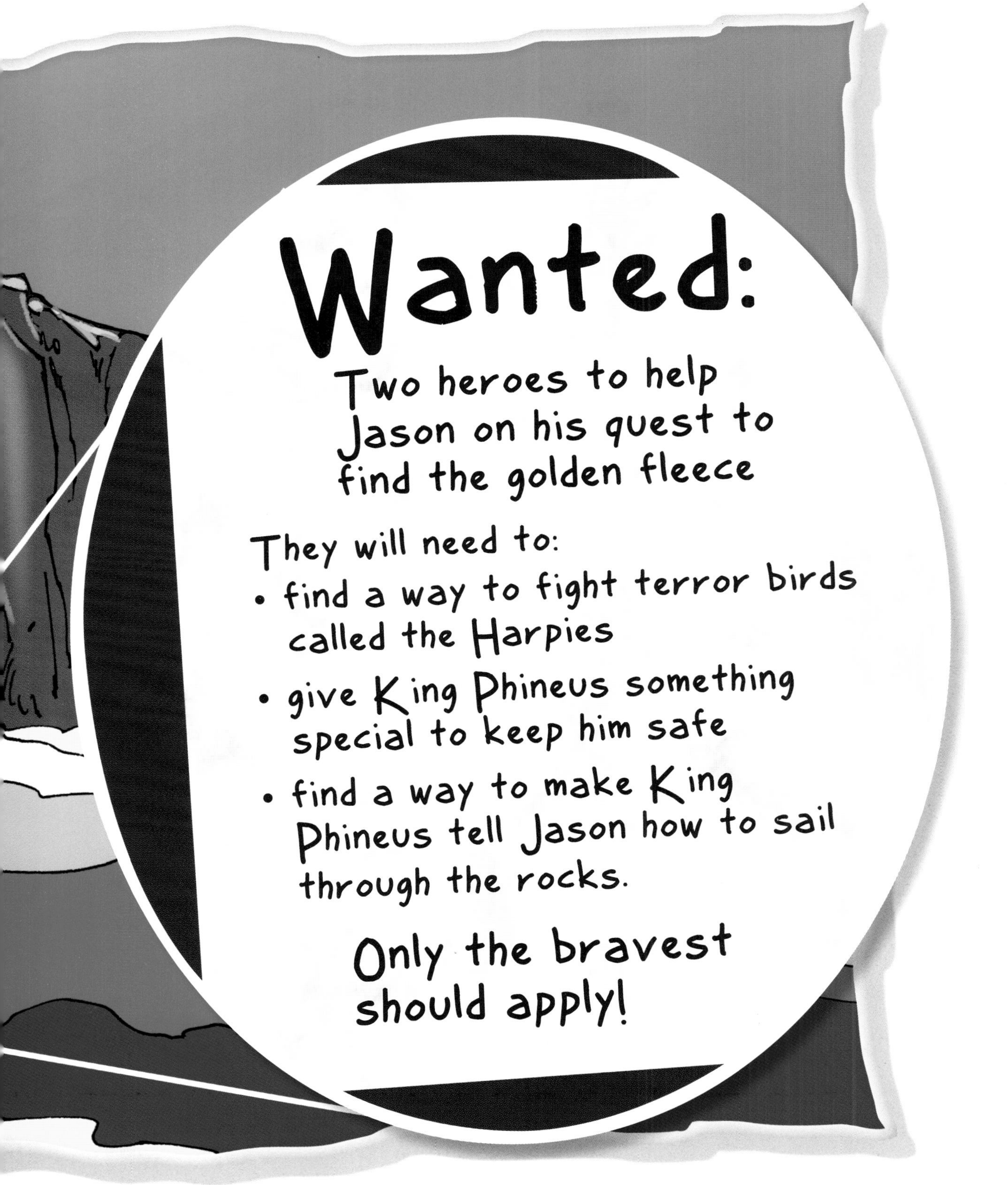
Wanted:
Two heroes to help Jason on his quest to find the golden fleece
They will need to:
• find a way to fight terror birds called the Harpies
• give King Phineus something special to keep him safe
• find a way to make King Phineus tell Jason how to sail through the rocks.
Only the bravest should apply!

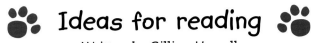

Ideas for reading

Written by Gillian Howell
Primary Literacy Consultant

Learning objectives: *(reading objectives correspond with Purple band; all other objectives correspond with Sapphire band)* read independently and with increasing fluency longer and less familiar texts; explore how writers use language for comic and dramatic effects; reflect on how working in role helps to explore complex issues

Curriculum links: History

Interest words: terror, whistle, umbrella, heroes, Argonauts, fleece, Harpies, horror, weapon, quest, bravery

Resources: pens, paper, internet

Word count: 714

Getting started

- Look at the cover and read the title together. Ask the children to describe what the illustration shows. Ask them to use adjectives to describe the two boys and the birds and predict what is happening to them.

- Turn to the back cover and read the blurb. Ask the children if they know what Ancient Greece means and explain if needed.

- Explain that this is a graphic novel with a large and important part of the plot told through the illustrations. Explain that they need to take careful notice of what is happening in the pictures.

Reading and responding

- Ask the children to read the story together. On p2, point out the speech bubbles and explain that reading them is an important part of reading the story. Allocate the roles of Jack, Sam, Jason, King Phineus and the narrator to different children and ask them to read their speech bubbles in an expressive tone.

- Remind the children to use their knowledge of letter sounds and context to help them work out new words, e.g. *whistle* on p2.

- As they read, pause at significant events and ask the children to say what they think will happen next before reading the next page, e.g. ask what do they think is happening to Jack and Sam at the end of p4 and what they think the boys thought when they found themselves in the sea on p5.

- Ask the children to read to the end of the story. Praise them for reading with expressive voices and support those who need extra help.